CHRISTMAS COOKING

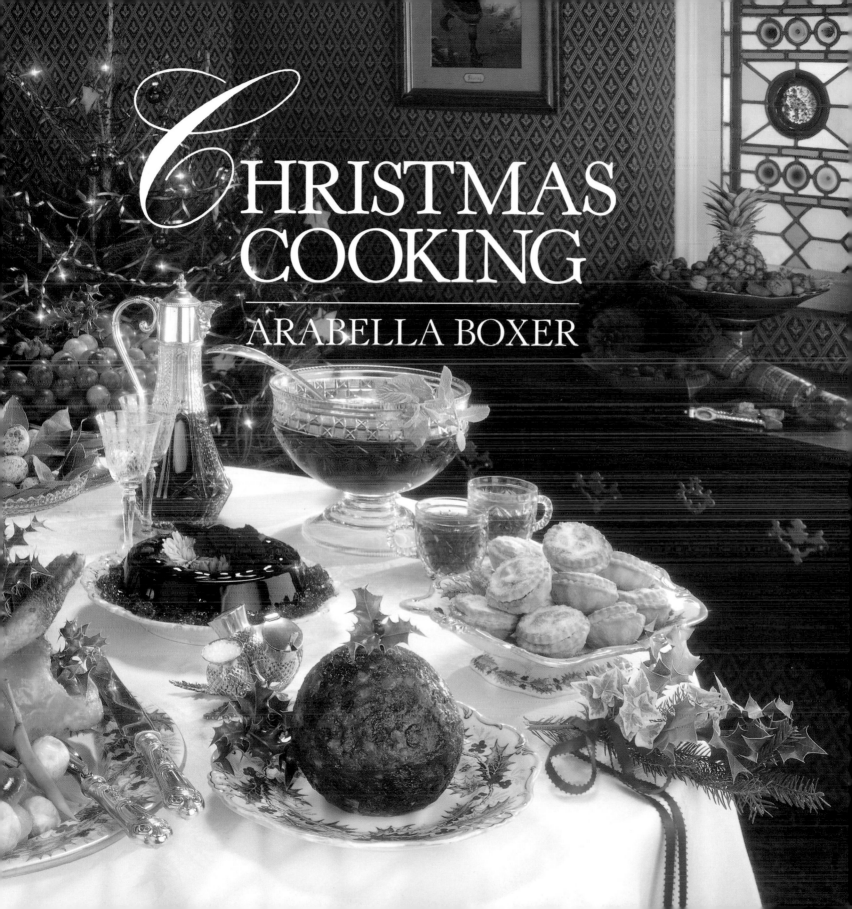

CHRISTMAS COOKING

ARABELLA BOXER

NOTE

1. All recipes serve four unless otherwise stated.

2. All spoon measurements are level. Spoon measures can be bought in both imperial and metric sizes to give accurate measurement of small quantities.

3. All eggs are sizes 2 or 3 unless otherwise stated.

4. All sugar is granulated unless otherwise stated.

5. Preparation times given are an average calculated during recipe testing.

6. Metric and imperial measurements have been calculated separately. Use one set of measurements only as they are not exact equivalents.

7. Cooking times may vary slightly depending on the individual oven. Dishes should be placed in the centre of an oven unless otherwise specified.

8. Always preheat the oven or grill to the specified temperature.

9. If using a fan-assisted oven, follow the manufacturer's instructions for guidance on temperature adjustments.

First published in Great Britain in 1988.
This edition published in 1996 by Hamlyn
an imprint of Reed Consumer Books Limited
Michelin House, 81 Fulham Road, London SW3 6RB
and Auckland, Melbourne, Singapore and Toronto

Recipe copyright © Arabella Boxer, 1975, 1980, 1981, 1983, 1988.
Copyright © 1988 additional text, photographs, illustrations, Reed International Books Limited.

ISBN 0 600 58953 6

A CIP catalogue record for this book is available from The British Library.

Produced by Mandarin Offset
Printed in Hong Kong

CONTENTS

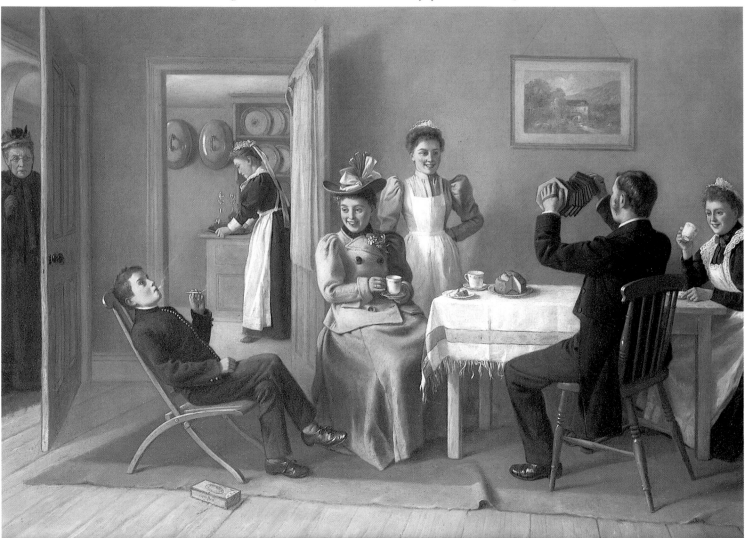

CHRISTMAS COUNTDOWN

Take the hard work out of Christmas cooking by preparing many essential foods in advance. This chapter contains a good range of recipes, including Christmas cake and plum pudding, pâtés, stuffings, ice creams and puddings, all of which will keep happily in freezer, refrigerator or store cupboard until needed.

PLUM PUDDING

MAKES 3 × 900 ml (1½ pint) PUDDINGS
750 g (1½ lb) seedless raisins, halved if large
225 g (8 oz) mixed candied peel, chopped
225 g (8 oz) glacé cherries, halved
100 g (4 oz) blanched almonds, chopped
350 g (12 oz) shredded suet
350 g (12 oz) soft white breadcrumbs
8 eggs beaten
150 ml (¼ pint) Guinness or other stout
6 tablespoons brandy
butter for greasing

To serve:
3 tablespoons brandy
sprig of holly

Preparation time: 45 minutes, plus
standing
Cooking time: 6 hours, plus 4–6 hours
before serving

This is the pudding I always make for Christmas, usually in late October or early November; it is unusual in that it contains neither flour nor sugar, and it makes an extremely good pudding. Those who like a very rich, moist pudding may not fancy it, but I find it quite rich enough.

Each of the three puddings which can be made from this mixture will serve 6–8 people, but if a larger pudding is needed the mixture can be divided between two larger bowls, or one very large one and one smaller one.

1. Mix well together the raisins, peel, cherries, almonds, suet and breadcrumbs. Stir in the well-beaten eggs, the stout and the brandy. The mixture can be left at this stage for a few hours, or even until the next day as this allows the flavours to develop, and the mixing and the cooking together make a long day's work.

2. Butter well three 1½ pint pudding basins and divide the pudding mixture among them. (Charms should be added at this stage if used; they are hard to find nowadays but may still be found in some department stores and speciality suppliers. If one pudding has charms, remember to distinguish it in some way, as weeks later it may be impossible to remember

which it was.) The bowls should not be filled too full; there should be a good inch left empty at the top.

3. Cover with a piece of buttered aluminium foil and wrap in a clean piece of white linen – part of an old sheet will do. Have a very large pan ready with enough boiling water to come halfway up the bowls. Lay each bowl carefully on an upturned saucer – use old chipped ones as the long boiling destroys the surface of the china – and cover the pan. Bring quickly back to the boil and keep boiling steadily for 6 hours, adding more boiling water as needed to keep the level up – roughly once an hour.

4. When the time is up, lift out the puddings and leave to cool: if they are not all needed at Christmas, one can be eaten straightaway. The others should be stored in a cool place as soon as they are cold.

5. On Christmas Day the pudding should be boiled again in the same way, for 4–6 hours.

6. To serve, turn out on to a heated dish, stick a small sprig of holly in the top, and pour some flaming brandy over it just before bringing it to the table. (Heat 3 tablespoons brandy gently in a saucepan, then set light to it.)

BRANDY BUTTER

SERVES 6
100 g (4 oz) unsalted butter
100 g (4 oz) caster sugar
3–4 tablespoons brandy

Preparation time: 15 minutes

LEFT, Brandy butter; RIGHT, Plum pudding

The traditional accompaniment to Christmas pudding, Brandy butter is also delicious served with rich fruit puddings and with mince pies. Make it a week before Christmas.

1. Cream the butter and the sugar together until smooth and pale in colour. Add the brandy gradually, beating the mixture after each addition.

2. Pile the brandy butter into a jar and chill in the refrigerator until needed.

Variation: for Rum butter, replace the brandy with an equal quantity of rum.

CHRISTMAS BREAD

MAKES 2 × 1 kg (2 lb) LOAVES
750 g (1¾ lb) plain flour
1 teaspoon salt
25 g (1 oz) fresh yeast or 15 g (½ oz) dried yeast
2 tablespoons tepid water
75 g (3 oz) lard
2 eggs
approx 175 ml (6 fl oz) milk, warmed
225 g (8 oz) raisins
100 g (4 oz) currants
100 g (4 oz) sultanas
50 g (2 oz) cut mixed peel
175 g (6 oz) sugar
1 tablespoon black treacle
1 teaspoon mixed ground nutmeg, cloves and cinnamon

Preparation time: 45 minutes, plus standing and rising
Cooking time: 1¼ hours
Oven: 180°C, 350°F, Gas Mark 4

Rosie's Robin.

This delicious spiced fruit bread will keep well wrapped in a cloth and stored in a tin. It is excellent with butter for tea. I make it instead of a Christmas cake, which seems to me too like Christmas pudding.

1. Put the flour in a large bowl with the salt and leave in a warm place. Put the yeast in a cup with the water and leave in the same warm place for 10 minutes.

2. Cut the lard in small pieces and rub into the flour. Beat the eggs and add the tepid milk and enough water to make up to 450 ml (¾ pint). Make a well in the middle of the flour and tip in first the yeast, then the eggs mixture. Mix roughly and put back in the warm place to rise for 30 minutes.

3. Meanwhile, measure all the dried fruit and put in another bowl in the warmth. When the ½ hour is up, turn out the flour mixture and knead well, then mix in the dried fruit, the sugar, treacle and spices. Mix thoroughly, then leave to rise again for 2 hours, or until the dough has risen to the top of the tin.

4. Butter and sprinkle with flour 2 × 1 kg (2 lb) loaf tins. (Line with greased greaseproof paper as well, if liked, to be on the safe side.)

5. Divide the mixture between the loaf tins.

6. Return to the warmth for 20 minutes, then cook in a preheated oven for 1¼ hours. The loaves are cooked when a skewer inserted into the centre of the loaves comes out clean.

7. Cool in the tins on a wire tray.

8. When quite cold, wrap in a clean cloth and store in an air-tight tin. The bread will keep for 2 weeks in a cool place.

BREAD AT CHRISTMAS TIME
The delicious spiced bread on this page is very much in the tradition of the richly spiced and fruit-laden breads and cakes served at Christmas for generations. But freshly baked basic bread is also an essential part of Christmas, so if you have a freezer, it is a good idea to bake a few loaves of basic bread a week or two before Christmas and freeze them. You will thus avoid the stale bread which is otherwise inevitable by the third day of the Christmas holiday, while a fresh, crusty loaf of homemade bread will turn a simple pâté and salad into a delicious meal.

CHESTNUT STUFFING

500 g (1 lb 4 oz) chestnuts
200 ml (⅓ pint) milk
a bunch of parsley
250 g (9 oz) belly of pork
250 g (9 oz) lean pork, from the leg
100 g (4 oz) shallots, peeled and chopped
1 clove garlic, peeled and chopped
1 tablespoon brandy
½ tablespoon sea salt
freshly ground black pepper
ground mace

Preparation time: 30 minutes, plus cooling
Cooking time: 12 minutes

This recipe makes quite a rich stuffing, ideal for filling the neck of a turkey, or the body of a large chicken or capon. Alternatively, it can be formed into small balls and fried, to serve around the bird as a garnish. Make it a day or two before you need it and store in the refrigerator.
1. Shell the chestnuts (see Chestnut soup, page 33), and simmer in the milk for 12 minutes; drain and cool.
2. Chop the parsley to give about 4 tablespoons and reserve until needed.
3. Chop the pork finely and put in a bowl. Then chop the chestnuts coarsely and stir into the pork. Stir the parsley, shallots and garlic into the mixture.
4. Add the brandy, salt, pepper, and a little ground mace.
5. Cook a small ball of the mixture in a frying pan to check the seasoning, and adjust as required.

PHEASANT AND CHESTNUT PÂTÉ

SERVES 12–16
1 oven-ready pheasant
750 g (1½ lb) belly of pork, or other cut of fat pork, minced
100 g (4 oz) fat unsmoked bacon, minced
2 cloves garlic, peeled and crushed
1 dessertspoon sea salt
10 black peppercorns
10 juniper berries, crushed
150–175 g (5–6 oz) cooked chestnuts (allow 225 g (8 oz) raw chestnuts)
a little stock or water
2 tablespoons brandy
175 ml (6 fl oz) red or white wine
some thin strips of bacon fat
melted lard, to cover

Preparation time: 40 minutes, plus cooling and weighting
Cooking time: 1¾–2 hours
Oven: 200°C, 400°F, Gas Mark 6; then 160°C, 325°F, Gas Mark 3

LEFT, Chestnut stuffing; RIGHT, Pheasant and chestnut pâté

If giving these pâtés as Christmas presents, they can be made to look especially pretty by decorating them with a sprig of holly, made of small bay leaves and cranberries, which you put in the bottom of the dish before piling on the pâté mixture.
1. Put the pheasant in a moderately hot oven for 15 minutes, then leave to cool. Cut the meat off the bones and chop it finely by hand. Reserve the carcass and a few scraps of meat for Game soup (page 33).
2. Mix the chopped pheasant with the minced meats and add the garlic, salt, peppercorns and the juniper berries which you have crushed roughly in a mortar. Put aside for the flavours to develop while you prepare the chestnuts.
3. Shell the chestnuts (see page 33) and put the nuts in a small pan with the stock or water, and cook for about 8 minutes till tender. Drain and cool. Chop them roughly when they have cooled and add to the meat mixture. Mix thoroughly and add the brandy and the wine.
4. Check the seasoning by frying a tiny ball of the mixture in butter and adjust if necessary. It should be quite highly seasoned; there is nothing worse than a bland pâté.
5. Decorate two ovenproof dishes (or moulds) with the strips of bacon fat and divide the mixture between the two. Cook them in a preheated moderate oven in a baking tin half filled with water, uncovered, for 1¼–1½ hours. When cooked, the pâtés will have shrunk away from the sides of the dishes. Leave to cool for a couple of hours, then weight with some kitchen weights, heavy tins, etc. The next day, store in the refrigerator, where they will keep for a week, or months, if they have a completely airtight seal of melted lard poured over them.
6. To serve, remove the fat and turn the pâtés out on to a dish with their jelly round them. Serve with toast, or home-made bread. Each pâté will serve 6–8. Alternatively, one large pâté can be made, increasing the cooking time by about 20 minutes.

DUCK PÂTÉ

SERVES 8

1 duck approx. 1.5 kg (3½ lb)
350 g (12 oz) fat pork; belly or throat, minced
350 g (12 oz) veal, minced
100 g (4 oz) fat mild bacon, minced
10 black peppercorns, crushed
½ tablespoon sea salt
½ teaspoon mace
1 clove garlic, peeled and crushed
175 ml (6 fl oz) dry white wine
2 tablespoons brandy
2 small oranges

Preparation time: 40 minutes, plus cooling and weighting
Cooking time: 1½–1¾ hours, plus 25 minutes to cook the duck
Oven: 190°C, 375°F, Gas Mark 5; then 160°C, 325°F, Gas Mark 3

This pâté will keep perfectly well in the refrigerator for one week. If the top is completely sealed with lard, so that it is air-tight, it will keep for several months.

1. Setting aside the liver for later, cook the duck for 25 minutes in a moderately hot oven, then remove it from the oven and leave to cool. When quite cold, cut all the flesh off the bones, removing the skin, and chop finely by hand.
2. Chop the raw duck liver and put it in a bowl with the chopped duck, minced meats, peppercorns, salt, mace and the garlic.
3. Moisten with the white wine and brandy, add the juice of 1 orange and mix everything well together.
4. To check the seasoning, fry a tiny ball of the mixture in butter and adjust if necessary. If possible, leave the mixture for an hour or two for the flavours to merge.
5. Peel the remaining orange and slice it thinly. Lay three or four of the slices in the bottom of your tin or dish and spoon the pâté mixture on top, flattening it with a palette knife. Cook in a baking tin half full of water in a preheated oven for 1½–1¾ hours. When cooked, the pâté will have shrunk away from the sides of the tin. (Alternatively, divide the mixture between two tins and cook for 1¼–1½ hours.)
6. Leave the pâté to cool then weight with two 1 kg (2 lb) weights, side by side. Put in the refrigerator when cold and leave for at least one day before eating.

PURÉE OF ROOT VEGETABLES

450 g (1 lb) of either turnips, swedes,
*   parsnips, or celeriac*
25 g (1 oz) butter
sea salt
freshly ground black pepper
75 ml (2½ fl oz) double cream
2 tablespoons chopped parsley

Preparation time: 10 minutes
Cooking time: 12–15 minutes

LEFT, Duck pâté; RIGHT, Purée of root vegetables

These vegetable purées make delicious accompaniments for roast or grilled lamb. They will keep in the refrigerator for 2–3 days after making.

1. Clean the vegetable of your choice and cut in chunks. Cook until tender in lightly salted water; drain well and dry out over gentle heat.
2. Process the vegetable in a blender or food processor until a smooth purée, then return it to the clean pan and stir over a low heat until most of the moisture has evaporated.
3. Add the butter in small bits, salt and pepper, and the cream. Finally, stir in the chopped parsley and serve.

SAUSAGE AND CHESTNUT STUFFING

450 g (1 lb) pure pork sausagemeat
450 g (1 lb) chestnuts
200 ml (⅓ pint) milk
100 g (4 oz) shallots, peeled and finely
    chopped
1 clove garlic, peeled and finely chopped
4 tablespoons finely chopped parsley
1 tablespoon brandy
1 dessertspoon sea salt
freshly ground black pepper
ground mace or nutmeg
milk, to mix

Preparation time: about 35 minutes, plus
cooling
Cooking time: 8–10 minutes

This mixture, which is sufficient to stuff a small turkey or capon, is also delicious made into small balls and fried, to serve with turkey, chicken or game.
1. Mash the sausagemeat in a deep bowl.
2. Shell the chestnuts (see page 33) and simmer in the milk for 8–10 minutes till tender. Drain and cool. Chop them coarsely and mix with the sausagemeat.
3. Add the shallots, garlic, parsley, brandy, sea salt, plenty of freshly ground black pepper and a little mace or nutmeg. A little milk may be necessary to bind the mixture together.

4. When the mixture is well blended together test for seasoning by frying a small ball of it in butter and adjust if necessary.

BREAD STUFFING

TO STUFF A 5.5 kg (12 lb) TURKEY
350 g (12 oz) shallots (or 225 g (8 oz) onions),
    finely chopped
100 g (4 oz) butter
350 g (12 oz) soft white breadcrumbs
40 g (1½ oz) chopped parsley
sea salt
freshly ground black pepper

Preparation time: 20 minutes, plus
cooling
Cooking time: 3–4 minutes

This traditional turkey stuffing is also good with chicken. Use half the quantity to stuff a large chicken.
1. Fry the shallots or onions gently in the butter until golden. Add the breadcrumbs and stir round until well mixed.
2. Remove from the heat and stir in the chopped parsley. Season with plenty of salt and black pepper.
3. Leave the stuffing to cool before using.

STORING STUFFINGS
The two stuffings on this page, and the Chestnut stuffing on page 13, will all keep for a week in the refrigerator, if kept in covered containers. They may also be frozen for up to four weeks. Thaw them completely before using, however, allowing 4 – 6 hours' thawing time.

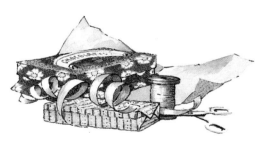

FROM THE TOP: Sausage and chestnut stuffing, Bread stuffing

CRANBERRY SAUCE

MAKES APPROX 1.2 l (2 pints)
450 g (1 lb) cranberries
450 ml (¾ pint) water
225 g (8 oz) sugar
1 tablespoon orange juice

Preparation time: about 10 minutes, plus standing and cooling
Cooking time: 8–10 minutes

This excellent sauce, with its tart fresh taste, is served cold, with hot or cold roast turkey, capon or ham. This recipe makes a large amount, which can be stored in the refrigerator over the Christmas holiday period. It could, of course, be made in half quantities.

1. Wash and pick over the cranberries. Bring the water and the sugar to the boil and add the berries. Bring back to the boil and simmer for about 3 minutes, till the berries start to burst. Turn off the heat and cover the pan.

2. Let the sauce stand for a few minutes, then pour it into a bowl and add the orange juice.

3. Leave to cool so that the sauce will thicken somewhat.

PINEAPPLE SORBET

SERVES 5–6
1 large pineapple
100 g (4 oz) sugar
120 ml (4 fl oz) water
juice of 4 medium oranges
1 tablespoon lime juice or 2 teaspoons lemon juice
2 egg whites

Preparation time: about 30 minutes, plus cooling and freezing
Cooking time: about 15 minutes

1. Cut the top and bottom off the pineapple and slice it thickly. Remove the central core from each slice and cut off the rind. Cut the slices in cubes and purée them in a food processor or blender. Push through a nylon sieve. You should have about 300 ml (½ pint).

2. Heat the sugar with the water in a heavy pan. Boil it gently until reduced to 150 ml (¼ pint) thin syrup and then cool.

3. Mix the orange juice with the pineapple purée and the cooled sugar syrup, adding the lime juice or the lemon juice to sharpen the flavour slightly.

4. Pour into an ice-cream machine and freeze for about 1 hour or until mushy. Tip into a bowl. Beat the egg whites until stiff and add them to the mixture in the bowl. Freeze again as usual. If you do not have an ice-cream machine, freeze the mixture in ice trays, covered with foil. Add the egg whites as above when the mixture is semi-frozen. Return to the freezer until set.

LEFT, Cranberry sauce; RIGHT, Pineapple sorbet

MINCEMEAT

MAKES ABOUT 2.75 kg (6 lb)
2 large lemons
175 g (6 oz) grilled rump steak, finely
chopped or minced (optional)
350 g (12 oz) hard green apples, e.g. Granny
Smith, peeled, cored and chopped
350 g (12 oz) mixed candied peel, chopped if
necessary
350 g (12 oz) raisins
350 g (12 oz) currants
50 g (12 oz) sugar
350 g (12 oz) shredded suet
½ teaspoon grated or ground nutmeg
½ teaspoon ground cinnamon
½ teaspoon ground allspice
½ teaspoon ground cloves
¼ teaspoon sea salt
2–3 turns of the peppermill
175 ml (6 fl oz) brandy

Preparation time: 45 minutes, plus
standing time

This is a traditional American recipe for mincemeat, and includes a small proportion of finely ground beefsteak. This was formerly the practice in England also, but has been forgotten. Although it sounds strange, it gives the mincemeat a most delicious flavour and is not, in fact, recognisable as meat. If preferred, however, it can be left out. Once packed into preserving jars, the mincemeat will keep for several weeks, if stored in a cool place.
1. Pare the rind off the lemons thinly, using a potato peeler, and squeeze and reserve the juice. Chop the rind very finely, then transfer to a large bowl.
2. If using the steak, add it to the bowl.
3. Add the apples and candied peel, and mix all together in the bowl.
4. Add the dried fruit, sugar, suet, spices, salt and pepper. Finally, stir in the lemon juice and the brandy. Stir well, then leave, covered, for several hours before packing into clean jars.

MINCE PIES
Our traditional Christmas mince pies bear little resemblance to those enjoyed in medieval times. Back in the Middle Ages, mince pies were filled with minced meats, which might include pheasant, rabbit, chicken or pigeon meat, plus their livers and hearts, a sheep's kidney or two and various flavourings and spices. Mince pies, having been banned with other Christmas celebrations by the Puritans in Oliver Cromwell's time, came back into favour after the Restoration in 1660. Now, though, they were round rather than the traditional oblong shape, which had represented the Christ Child's crib. Their meat content also gradually changed until today it has virtually disappeared.

MINCE PIES

MAKES 12
butter, for greasing

Pastry:
175 g (6 oz) Philadelphia cheese
175 g (6 oz) butter
250 g (9 oz) plain flour, sifted
¾ teaspoon sugar
a pinch of salt

450 g (1 lb) mincemeat (see above)
beaten egg yolk, for brushing
caster sugar, for sprinkling

Preparation time: 25 minutes, plus chilling
Cooking time: 20 minutes
Oven: 190°C, 375°F, Gas Mark 5

These mince pies can be kept and reheated, but are not quite so good as soon after baking. If preferred, an ordinary short pastry can be used, but I find this one made with cream cheese particularly delicious.
1. Lightly grease 12 small round patty tins and set aside.
2. Blend the cream cheese and butter together well, then add the flour, sugar, and salt. Blend again, until the mixture forms a ball and clings together.
3. Wrap in cling film and chill for 45 minutes.
4. Roll out the pastry and line small round tins. Fill each one generously with mincemeat, doming it up slightly. Cover with a second layer of pastry and seal the edges

by damping them, then pinching together.
5. Brush with beaten egg yolk and bake in a preheated oven for 20 minutes, until golden brown.
6. Sprinkle with caster sugar on taking out of the oven and serve hot with brandy butter or thick cream.

LEFT, Mince pies; RIGHT, Mincemeat

VANILLA WHEATGERM ICE CREAM

SERVES 6
2 eggs + 2 egg yolks
75 g (3 oz) vanilla sugar or caster sugar
and ½ vanilla pod
300 ml (½ pint) milk
300 ml (½ pint) double cream
50 g (2 oz) sweetened wheatgerm

Preparation time: 20 minutes, plus standing (if necessary), cooling, freezing
Cooking time: about 15 minutes

1. If you have no vanilla sugar, put half a vanilla pod in the milk, heat to boiling point, cover, remove from heat, and leave for 20 minutes.
2. Beat the eggs and the egg yolks together with an electric beater. Add the vanilla sugar, or caster sugar, and continue to beat. Heat the milk until just about to boil, removing the vanilla pod if necessary, then pour on to the eggs and sugar. Continue to beat until incorporated.
3. Place the bowl over a pan of simmering water and stir constantly until very slightly thickened, like an egg custard. Then pour the mixture through a strainer into a clean bowl. Stand it in a sink half full of cold water and leave to cool, stirring now and then to prevent a skin forming.

4. Beat the cream until semi-whipped and fold it into the cooled custard. Pour into an ice-cream machine and freeze for an hour. Then stir in the wheatgerm and continue freezing. Alternatively, if you do not have an ice-cream machine, freeze the mixture in ice trays, covered with foil. After an hour, beat the mixture with a fork and add the wheatgerm before returning it to the freezer.

HAZELNUT ICE CREAM

SERVES 6
75 g (3 oz) vanilla sugar or caster sugar and
½ vanilla pod
300 ml (½ pint) milk
50 g (2 oz) hazelnuts, blanched
2 tablespoons caster sugar
2 eggs + 2 egg yolks
300 ml (½ pint) double cream

Preparation time: 20 minutes, plus standing, cooling and freezing
Cooking time: about 12 minutes

1. If you have no vanilla sugar, put half a vanilla pod into the milk and heat to boiling point. Cover the pan, remove from the heat, and stand for 20 minutes.
2. Put the hazelnuts in a heavy frying pan with the 2 tablespoons caster sugar and cook over a fairly strong heat, stirring constantly, until the sugar caramelizes. The nuts will turn a golden brown and the whole pan will smoke slightly.
3. Turn out on to an oiled surface – marble or glass is best – and leave to cool. Then put the hazelnuts into a food processor or blender and chop until reduced to a medium-fine consistency; an uneven texture does not matter, it even improves the ice cream.
4. Beat the eggs and the yolks with the vanilla sugar, or plain caster sugar, if used, until thick. Remove the vanilla pod from the milk, if necessary, and heat the milk until almost boiling. Pour on to the eggs, beating all the time.

5. Stand the bowl over a pan of simmering water and stir constantly until slightly thickened – about 8 minutes. Strain into a clean bowl and stand in a sink full of very cold water, stirring now and then to prevent a skin forming.
6. When cool, whip the cream until semi-thick and fold into the egg custard. Pour into an ice-cream machine and freeze. When almost frozen, fold in the crushed nut mixture and continue to freeze until totally set. If you have no ice-cream machine, freeze the mixture in ice trays, covered with foil. After about 1 hour, beat the mixture well with a fork, then fold in the crushed nuts carefully. Continue to freeze until set.

Variation: For Almond ice cream, substitute blanched almonds for the hazelnuts.

LEFT, Hazelnut ice cream; RIGHT, Vanilla wheatgerm ice cream

THE TWELVE DAYS OF CHRISTMAS

Here is a splendid collection of recipes, both traditional and modern, from which to create menus for the whole holiday period, from Christmas Eve to Epiphany.

GINGER CONSOMMÉ

SERVES 6–8
1st day:
2 duck or pheasant carcasses, or 1 of either
  plus 1 kg (2 lb) raw chicken joints
1 large onion, including skin, halved
3 leeks, halved
3 large carrots, halved
3 stalks celery, halved
1 large bay leaf
4 stalks parsley
1 tablespoon sea salt
15 black peppercorns
300 ml (½ pint) dry white wine

2nd day:
sea salt
freshly ground black pepper
a little lemon juice
2 l (3½ pints) water

To garnish:
4 spring onions
4 cm (1½ inch) piece fresh ginger
16 tiny sprigs watercress

Preparation time: 20 minutes, plus
leaving overnight
Cooking time: 2½–3 hours

This consommé can well be made in
conjunction with a game pâté, using the
carcasses of the birds cooked for the pâté.
1. Start a day or two in advance. Put the
carcasses and chicken joints (if using), in a
deep pot with the flavouring vegetables
and herbs, salt, peppercorns and wine.
Add the cold water and bring very slowly
to the boil. As it approaches boiling point,
remove the scum that rises to the surface.
After about 8 minutes this should have
become clear. Then cook gently, half
covered, for 2½–3 hours. Strain and leave
overnight.
2. Next day, remove the fat, tip the
consommé back into the pan and reheat.
Adjust the seasoning, adding salt and
pepper and a little lemon juice, to taste. If
the consommé seems too weak in flavour,
boil it up for a little to reduce. (You will
need 200 ml/⅓ pint per person.)
3. Transfer 300 ml (½ pint) of the
consommé to a small pan for cooking the
garnish. Cut the spring onions into very
thin strips about 4 cm (1½ inches) long.
Peel the ginger and cut in tiny cubes.
Shortly before serving heat the small pan
of consommé until simmering. Drop in
the spring onions and cook for 30 seconds,
then add the ginger and cook for another
30 seconds. Remove from the heat, and
drop in the little sprigs of watercress.
Reheat the big pan until it is almost
boiling, then stir in the contents of the
small pan, and serve, either in a tureen, or
in small cups. Divide the garnish evenly
between them.

BRUSSELS SPROUTS WITH CHESTNUTS

SERVES 5
250 g (9 oz) chestnuts
200 ml (⅓ pint) chicken stock
750 g (1 lb 8 oz) small Brussels sprouts
25 g (1 oz) butter
sea salt
freshly ground black pepper
sprigs fresh parsley, to garnish

Preparation time: 35 minutes, plus
cooling
Cooking time: about 15 minutes

Brussels sprouts cooked this way are very
good with roast turkey, game and chicken.
1. Make a small nick in the flat side of each
chestnut and cover with cold water. Bring
to the boil, then remove from the heat.
Shell the nuts, taking only a few at a time
out of the hot water. Reheat the pan if the
chestnuts get hard to shell.
2. When all the chestnuts are peeled,
put them in a small pan with the chicken
stock and cook gently, covered, for
about 12 minutes, until they are tender.
Drain, reserving the stock for adding to a
soup later, and allow the nuts to cool
slightly.
3. Meanwhile, boil the sprouts as usual,
keeping them very firm, then drain well
and dry out over gentle heat. Stir in the
butter, sea salt, and lots of black pepper.
4. Chop the chestnuts coarsely, then stir
them into the sprouts. Serve as soon as
possible garnished with parsley.

*LEFT, Ginger consommé; RIGHT, Brussels sprouts
with chestnuts*

ROAST TURKEY

SERVES 6–8

4.5–5.5 kg (10–12 lb) oven-ready turkey,
  with giblets
Sausage and chestnut stuffing (page 16)
1 onion, peeled and quartered (optional)
40 g (1½ oz) butter or margarine, softened
2 tablespoons vegetable oil
salt
freshly ground black pepper
watercress or parsley sprigs, to garnish

For the stock:
½ onion, peeled
water

Preparation time: about 30 minutes
Cooking time: 3–3½ hours
Oven: 180°C, 350°F, Gas Mark 4

I find a bird weighing 4.5–5.5 kg (10–12 lb) (after drawing) is a perfect size for a small party of six or seven people. Last year we were six, and a 4.5 kg (10 lb) bird was ideal. On Christmas Day itself, we only ate one side of the bird, leaving a whole side of the carcass intact to eat cold the following day.

1. Remove the giblets, liver, etc, sprinkle the inside of the bird with salt and pepper and stuff with the Sausage and chestnut stuffing, if liked, or simply put the onion in the inside.

2. Stuff the neck (gullet) end of the bird with the suggested stuffing, or with a different one, if preferred.

3. It is best to sew up the bird after stuffing it, but I usually put a small peeled onion in the mouth of the cavity, and tie the legs tightly round it.

4. The whole surface of the bird should then be generously rubbed with butter, and sprinkled with salt and pepper. Wrap a buttered sheet of aluminium foil around the bird, so that it is completely enclosed. Alternatively, the bird can be started off uncovered, and a piece of foil or grease-proof paper put over it when it is sufficiently browned.

5. Ideally it should then be laid on a rack in a roasting tin, but this is not vital. Add the oil to the tin. Roast the bird in a preheated oven for 3–3½ hours. Check if the bird is cooked by inserting a skewer into the thickest part of the thigh, when the juices should run clear. If pink, cook the turkey for a further 15 minutes and test again.

6. While the turkey is cooking, make a stock from the giblets, simmering them with half an onion in a pan of water for about 1 hour. [A]

7. Transfer the turkey to a large carving dish. Drain off the fat from the tin and use the juices and reserved giblet stock to make gravy.

8. Arrange the turkey on a large serving dish and surround with roast potatoes, chipolatas and bacon rolls. Garnish with watercress or parsley sprigs. Serve with Brussels sprouts, the gravy and Cranberry sauce (page 19) handed separately.

[A] The giblet stock may be prepared up to 24 hours in advance, strained and chilled.

BREAD SAUCE

¼ white loaf, 2–3 days old
350 ml (12 fl oz) milk
½ onion, peeled
2 cloves
½ bay leaf
sea salt
freshly ground black pepper
15 g (½ oz) butter
2 tablespoons single cream

Preparation time: 15 minutes, plus standing
Cooking time: about 12–15 minutes

This sauce is traditionally served with roast turkey or chicken.

1. Remove the crusts from the bread, cut into cubes and turn into breadcrumbs, either by hand or in a food processor. Put aside.

2. Put the milk in a small pan with the half onion stuck with the cloves, and the half bay leaf. Bring slowly to the boil, then remove from the heat and stand, covered, for 20 minutes.

3. Discard the onion and bay leaf and skim the milk. Reheat gently, until simmering, then shake in 5–6 tablespoons bread-crumbs gradually, stopping just before the desired thickness is reached, remembering that the sauce will thicken slightly on cooking. Simmer gently for 3 minutes, adding salt and pepper to taste. Remove from the heat, stir in the butter and cream and serve as soon as possible after making.

LEFT, Roast turkey with vegetable trimmings; RIGHT, Bread sauce

CHRISTMAS CAKE

MAKES 1 × 20 cm (8 inch) ROUND
CAKE
225 g (8 oz) butter
225 g (8 oz) soft brown sugar
2 tablespoons treacle
4 eggs
350 g (12 oz) plain flour, sifted
1 teaspoon baking powder
1½ teaspoons ground cloves
1½ teaspoons ground cinnamon
1½ teaspoons ground nutmeg
100 g (4 oz) ground almonds
225 g (8 oz) currants
225 g (8 oz) raisins
225 g (8 oz) sultanas
65 ml (2½ fl oz) milk
juice of 1 orange

Preparation time: 1 hour
Cooking time: 2½ hours
Oven: 160°C, 325°F, Gas Mark 3

This was my grandmother's recipe; a rich spiced fruit cake of this sort was often handed round with the cheese at luncheon parties in Scotland. It takes an hour to make and is quite tiring, but it can be made well in advance. It can be covered with almond paste and royal icing, in traditional Christmas style, or simply eaten as it is.

1. Grease well a 20 cm (8 inch) round cake tin. (To make smaller rectangular cakes, use two tins measuring roughly 20 × 10 cm (8 × 4 inch).)
2. Cream the butter and beat in the sugar gradually. Stir in the treacle, mixing well.
3. Break one egg at a time into a cup, beat with a fork, then mix into the creamed butter and sugar. Fold in a spoonful of flour after each egg to prevent curdling.
4. When all the eggs are incorporated, add the baking powder and the spices to the remaining flour and fold into the mixture. Stir in the ground almonds, then the currants, raisins and sultanas. Last of all, stir in the milk and the orange juice.
5. Put the mixture into the prepared tin (or smaller tins, if preferred), and place in the centre of a preheated oven.
6. Bake for 2½ hours. After 1 hour cover the tins loosely with a piece of aluminium foil to prevent the cakes from getting too brown.
7. Cool the cake in the tin for a few minutes, then remove from the tin and rest on a wire tray until completely cooled. Store in an airtight tin until required.
8. For notes on icing with almond paste and Royal icing see pages 134–6.

CHRISTMAS PUDDING

SERVES 8–10
butter, for greasing
100 g (4 oz) soft white breadcrumbs
225 g (8 oz) shredded suet
225 g (8 oz) currants
225 g (8 oz) raisins
100 g (4 oz) sugar
50 g (2 oz) candied peel
grated rind of ½ lemon
½ teaspoon ground nutmeg
½ teaspoon mixed spice
a pinch of salt
4 eggs, beaten
a liqueur glass of brandy
3 tablespoons brandy, to serve
sprig of holly, to decorate

Preparation time: 30 minutes
Cooking time: 4–6 hours, plus re-steaming before serving

This recipe makes a delicious, light, moist pudding, less firm than the usual plum pudding. It stores well, making resteaming on Christmas Day easy. It is also excellent for a winter's weekend lunch party, served with a custard sauce.

1. Butter well a 1.5 l (2½ pint) pudding basin and set aside.
2. Mix all the ingredients except for the eggs and the brandy in a large deep bowl.
3. When very thoroughly mixed, stir in the eggs. Mix in the brandy and put the mixture in the prepared pudding basin.
4. Cover with aluminium foil or a cloth and boil or steam for 4–6 hours.
5. On Christmas Day, re-steam the pudding for 3–4 hours.
6. To serve, turn out on to a warmed plate, decorate with holly and pour flaming brandy over it (see page 7).

LEFT, Christmas cake, with rough icing; RIGHT, Christmas pudding

GAME SOUP WITH LENTILS

SERVES 6–8

1 pheasant carcass, raw if possible
2 onions, peeled and halved
2 carrots
1 leek
2 stalks celery
1 bay leaf
sea salt
freshly ground black pepper
3 tablespoons olive oil
250 g (9 oz) green or brown lentils

Preparation time: 35 minutes, plus cooling
Cooking time: 2–4 hours

1. Pick off any scraps of meat you can get from the carcass and reserve.
2. Put the bones in a pressure cooker with 1 halved onion, 1 halved carrot, the green part of the leek and the ends of the celery. Add the bay leaf, salt and pepper. Pour on 1.5 litres (2½ pints) cold water, bring to the boil, and cook under pressure for 1 hour. Alternatively, use 1.75 litres (3 pints) water and cook for 3 hours in an ordinary pan.
3. Strain and cool, then remove any fat from the surface.
4. Chop the remaining onion, carrot, leek and celery. Heat the oil in a heavy pan and cook the chopped vegetables slowly for 8 minutes, stirring frequently. Add the washed lentils and stir around until they are coated with fat.
5. Reheat the stock and add to the pan. Bring to the boil slowly, removing any scum which forms on the surface. Simmer gently for 45 minutes, or until the lentils are soft.
6. Cut the scraps of pheasant into neat dice and stir into the soup before serving; if using raw pheasant, allow 5 minutes simmering to cook them. Add salt and pepper to taste.

CHESTNUT SOUP

SERVES 5 6

250 g (9 oz) chestnuts
1 medium onion, peeled
1 medium carrot, scrubbed
1 medium leek, washed
1 stalk celery, washed
1.2 litres (2 pints) stock: turkey, duck, game or chicken
sea salt
freshly ground black pepper
1 cooking apple, peeled, cored and chopped
2–3 tablespoons finely chopped parsley, to garnish

Preparation time: 35 minutes, plus cooling
Cooking time: 45–50 minutes

1. Using a small sharp knife, make a nick in the flat side of each chestnut. Put them in a pan and cover with cold water. Bring to the boil, then remove from the heat. Lift out three or four nuts at a time and cut off the shells, removing the inner skin at the same time. When this becomes difficult, reheat the pan of water and chestnuts until almost boiling.
2. Slice the onion, carrot, leek and celery. Put them in a pan with the whole nuts and cover with the cold stock. Add salt and pepper and bring slowly to the boil. Simmer gently for 30 minutes, then add the apple.
3. Simmer for another 10 minutes, then cool slightly.
4. Purée the soup in a blender or food processor and return to the cleaned pan. Reheat, check for taste and add more salt and pepper as needed.
5. Sprinkle the soup with chopped parsley just before serving.

TOP, Game soup with lentils; BOTTOM, Chestnut soup

CURRIED CREAM OF CHICKEN SOUP

SERVES 6

25 g (1 oz) butter
1 teaspoon mild curry powder
2 tablespoons plain flour
600 ml (1 pint) strong home made chicken stock, heated
juice of ½ lemon
150 ml (¼ pint) single cream
sea salt
freshly ground black pepper
1 chicken breast, poached and cubed

Preparation time: 15 minutes
Cooking time: 10 minutes

This is an exquisite soup, quite rich, and an elegant start to a dinner party. I usually poach a chicken especially, using the stock and one breast for the soup, and the rest of the bird for a chicken salad, or chicken pancakes.

1. Melt the butter in a heavy saucepan, add the curry powder and cook for 2 minutes over a low heat, stirring. Add the flour and continue to stir for another 3 minutes.

2. Remove from the heat and start adding the heated stock, stirring until it is blended. Replace over the heat and stir for 4–5 minutes.

3. Remove from the heat and add the lemon juice, cream, and salt and pepper to taste. Add the chicken breast to the soup a few minutes before serving. Pour the soup into cups or bowls, ensuring the chicken breast is evenly distributed in each one.

BEAN SOUP

SERVES 6

175 g (6 oz) dried haricot beans (cannellini or soissons if possible)
1 onion, peeled and chopped
2 carrots, scrubbed and chopped
2 leeks, trimmed and sliced
2 stalks celery, chopped
225 g (8 oz) tomatoes, skinned and chopped
4 tablespoons olive oil
1.5 l (2½ pint) game stock, or the bean stock mixed with some chicken stock
1 level dessertspoon sea salt
freshly ground black pepper
4 tablespoons chopped parsley

Preparation time: 25 minutes, plus soaking
Cooking time: about 1 hour 10 minutes

When made in conjunction with a game pâté, using the carcass of the almost raw pheasant for the stock, this is the best soup imaginable. Otherwise it can be made perfectly well with chicken stock, or simply with the cooking liquor from the beans made up to the right amount with half a stock cube added.

1. Soak the dried beans for 2–3 hours, then put them in enough fresh water to cover generously, cook rapidly for 10 minutes, then gently until soft. Drain them and reserve the stock.

2. Heat the oil in a flameproof casserole and cook the onion in it slowly until slightly softened. Add the carrots, then the leeks, then the celery. Add the tomatoes last of all.

3. Heat the stock and pour on. Bring to the boil and simmer gently for about 25 minutes, till the vegetables are soft without being mushy. Stir in the beans and re-heat. Add salt and pepper to taste, and stir in the chopped parsley just before serving.

LEFT, Curried cream of chicken soup; RIGHT, Bean soup

PARSNIP SOUP

*100 g (4 oz) streaky bacon rashers, rinded
and diced
40 g (1½ oz) butter
1 large onion, peeled and chopped
2 stalks celery, chopped
450 g (1 lb) parsnips, peeled and diced
1 bay leaf
sea salt
freshly ground black pepper
1½ tablespoons plain flour
600 ml (1 pint) creamy milk
sprigs fresh chervil, to garnish*

Preparation time: 25 minutes
Cooking time: about 20 minutes

1. Fry the bacon gently in 25 g (1 oz) of the butter in a heavy pan. Allow about 10 minutes slow frying for the bacon to render all its fat and become crisp. Add the onion to the bacon, adding a little extra fat if necessary. Cook gently, stirring often for another 8–10 minutes, till the onion has softened.
2. Add the celery to the pan and cook for another 6–8 minutes – the chopped parsnips cook so quickly that the other vegetables must be three-quarters cooked before adding them, otherwise the soup will become mushy before the onion and celery are tender.
3. Add the parsnips to the celery and onion and barely cover with hot water. Add a bay leaf, sea salt and black pepper, remembering the bacon is already salty, and simmer for 10–12 minutes, till the parsnips have become soft.
4. Mix the flour to a paste in a cup with a little of the milk and stir into the soup. Simmer for 2 minutes till slightly thickened, then heat the rest of the milk and pour on. When all is well mixed and hot, stir in the remaining 15 g (½ oz) butter, and serve garnished with fresh chervil.

SMOKED SALMON PÂTÉ

SERVES 2–3
*100 g (4 oz) smoked salmon pieces (trimmings
    are ideal for this dish)
50 g (2 oz) unsalted butter
2 tablespoons double cream
freshly ground black pepper
cayenne pepper
lemon juice
sprig of parsley, to garnish*

Preparation time: 25 minutes, plus chilling

1. Chop the smoked salmon, removing all hard pieces, bones, etc. Pound in a mortar or process in a blender till smooth, then add the butter cut in small pieces. The butter should be cool and firm, but not too hard.
2. When all is amalgamated into a smooth paste, add the cream, plenty of freshly ground black pepper, cayenne and lemon juice to taste.
3. Turn into a small dish and chill for several hours.
4. Serve garnished with a sprig of parsley, or perhaps a curl of smoked salmon, and with hot toast. Parsley butter adds a pretty touch.

LEFT AND TOP, Parsnip soup; RIGHT, Smoked salmon pâté

SMOKED HADDOCK MOUSSE

1 carrot, scrubbed and sliced
1 onion, peeled and quartered
1 leek, sliced
6 peppercorns
salt
3 stalks parsley
1 bay leaf
2 large smoked haddocks
15 g (½ oz) gelatine
2 tablespoons lemon juice
cayenne pepper
300 ml (½ pint) double cream

Preparation time: 30 minutes, plus chilling
Cooking time: about 55 minutes

1. For a court bouillon, put the carrot, onion and leek in cold water in a fairly large pan with the peppercorns and some salt, the parsley stalks and bay leaf, and bring to the boil. Simmer for 30 minutes.
2. Cut the haddocks in quarters and poach in the court bouillon for 12 minutes, then lift out and drain.
3. Continue to boil up the court bouillon until well flavoured and reduced, without allowing it to become too salty. Use 65 ml (2½ fl oz) of it to dissolve the gelatine.

4. Flake the fish, discarding all skin and bone, and weigh it. You should have about 450 g (1 lb). Put it in the blender with 200 ml (⅓ pint) of the reduced court bouillon. Blend till smooth, adding lemon juice, cayenne pepper, and extra salt if required. Stir in the dissolved gelatine. Beat the cream and fold it in. Pour into a soufflé dish and chill in the refrigerator.

SEVICHE OF SCALLOPS WITH HERBS

10 large scallops
150 ml (¼ pint) lemon juice
1½ tablespoons chopped shallot
½ tablespoon chopped tarragon
½ tablespoon chopped dill
½ tablespoon chopped chives
½ tablespoon chopped parsley
1½ tablespoons sunflower-seed oil

Preparation time: 35 minutes, plus marinating

Scallops are often sold off their shells nowadays, expecially in supermarkets. Shells are not essential to this delicious recipe, of course; just serve the seviche on small, pretty serving plates if you prefer.
1. Detach the scallops from their shells and scrape off the beard-like fringe and intestinal thread. Cut away the orange flesh. Wash the white parts and pat dry. Cut in slices about 5mm (¼ inch) thick. Wash and prepare the coral in the same way, if you like.
2. Choose 4 medium shells, scrub them well and leave to drain.
3. Put the sliced scallops in a bowl and pour over the lemon juice. (There should be enough almost to cover them.) Cover with cling film and put in the refrigerator for 24 hours, stirring occasionally, so that the scallops are well marinated.

4. When ready to serve, chop the shallots and herbs very finely indeed. Drain off the lemon juice from the scallops and stir in the oil. Add the shallots and herbs and mix well. Spoon on to the shells and serve immediately as a first course, with thinly sliced brown bread and butter.

TOP, Smoked haddock mousse; BOTTOM, Seviche of scallops with herbs

STEAMED BASS WITH GINGER

1 × 750 g–1 kg (1½–2 lb) bass, gutted and
 cleaned
1 teaspoon sugar
1 teaspoon sea salt
½ tablespoon sesame oil
½ tablespoon soy sauce
8 thin slices fresh ginger
2 garlic cloves, peeled and thinly sliced
4 spring onions, peeled and sliced

Sauce:
2 tablespoons dry vermouth
2 tablespoons sunflower oil
1 tablespoon sesame oil
1 tablespoon soy sauce

To garnish:
4 spring onions

Preparation time: 25 minutes
Cooking time: 25 minutes

1. Rub the fish inside and out with the sugar, salt, sesame oil and soy sauce. Oil a piece of foil and lay half the sliced ginger, garlic and spring onions on it. Lay the fish on this, and cover with the remaining ginger, garlic, and spring onions. Wrap the foil round the fish and seal it tightly.
2. Have some water boiling fiercely in the bottom half of a steamer, or wok. Lay the wrapped fish on the top part of the steamer, or on a rack, cover with the lid, and steam steadily for 25 minutes, replenishing the water as required.
3. While the fish is cooking, mix the ingredients for the sauce in a small jug.
4. For the garnish, cut the spring onions into 5 cm (2 inch) sections, then cut each section into thin slivers.
5. When the fish is ready, unwrap it and pour any juices into the sauce. Slide the fish on to a flat dish, discarding the ginger, garlic, and spring onions. Take the skin off the top side of the fish and pour the sauce over, after mixing it well. Garnish with the strips of spring onion. Serve the bass with plain boiled potatoes and a green salad.

Variation: When bass is not available, a large piece of halibut or turbot, a whole grey mullet, or large (farmed) trout, may be used instead.

BAKED HALIBUT PARCELS

olive oil
4 halibut steaks, about 225 g (8 oz) each
sea salt
freshly ground black pepper
100 g (4 oz) shallots, peeled and finely
 chopped
675 g (1½ lb) tomatoes, skinned and chopped
2 tablespoons chopped fresh rosemary

Preparation time: 15 minutes
Cooking time: 25 minutes
Oven: 180°C, 350°F, Gas Mark 4

1. Brush four pieces of foil with olive oil. Sprinkle the fish steaks with salt and pepper on each side and lay them on the foil.
2. Scatter the shallots over the fish and lay the tomatoes over the shallots. Sprinkle the chopped rosemary over the tomatoes. Dribble a little olive oil over each steak and wrap up the foil.
3. Put the parcels of foil on a rack in a roasting pan and bake in a preheated oven for 25 minutes. Serve with new potatoes and a green salad.

TOP, Steamed bass with ginger; BOTTOM, Baked halibut parcels

HERB SOUFFLÉ

40 g (1½ oz) butter
2 tablespoons plain flour
200 ml (⅓ pint) milk
sea salt
freshly ground black pepper
½ teaspoon Dijon mustard
50 g (2 oz) Gruyère cheese, grated
1 tablespoon chopped fresh burnet
3 egg yolks, lightly beaten
4 egg whites

Preparation time: 25 minutes, plus cooling
Cooking time: 30 minutes
Oven: 200°C, 400°F, Gas Mark 6

1. Melt the butter in a small saucepan, stir in the flour and cook over a low heat for 1 minute, stirring until smooth. Heat the milk and add it to the pan. Continue to cook over a low heat, stirring all the time, until the ingredients have blended into a smooth creamy sauce. Simmer gently for 3 minutes. Add salt and pepper to taste, and stir in the mustard, grated cheese and burnet.
2. Take off the heat and cool for a moment, then stir in the lightly beaten egg yolks. Cool for 5 minutes. Beat the egg whites until stiff, then fold them into the sauce. Turn into a buttered 900 ml (1½ pint) ovenproof soufflé dish and bake for 20 minutes in a preheated oven. Serve immediately.

TURBOT GRATIN

1 kg (2 lb) turbot
½ onion, peeled
1 carrot
1 stalk celery
1 bay leaf
1 teaspoon sea salt
6 black peppercorns
150 ml (¼ pint) white wine or 2 tablespoons
    white vinegar
50 g (2 oz) butter
2 tablespoons plain flour
300 ml (½ pint) single cream
2 tablespoons finely chopped parsley
    (optional)

Preparation time: 30 minutes, plus cooling
Cooking time: about 1½ hours
Oven (optional): 200°C, 400°F, Gas Mark 6

1. Put enough cold water to cover the fish in a large shallow pan or fish kettle. Do not put the fish in the pan yet. Add the flavouring vegetables and bay leaf, the salt and peppercorns. Add the wine (if there is none readily available you can substitute 2 tablespoons white wine vinegar) and bring slowly to the boil. Simmer for 30 minutes to flavour the court bouillon, then put in the fish. Poach very gently for about 20 minutes, or till it flakes easily with a fork.
2. Lift out the fish and boil up the stock to reduce and concentrate the flavour. Be careful it does not get too salty.
3. When the fish is cool enough to handle, remove the skin and bone and break the fish into pieces, or large flakes.
4. Melt the butter, stir in the flour, and cook for a minute or two. Strain 300 ml (½ pint) of the court bouillon and blend with the roux. Add the cream and taste for seasoning. Mix lightly with the fish and pour into a shallow gratin dish. Either serve immediately, sprinkled with the chopped parsley, or put in a moderately hot oven for 10 minutes to brown the dish slightly.

Variations: Substitute halibut for the turbot or, for a simpler, less expensive dish, use cod or haddock fillet, and a mixture of milk and water instead of the court bouillon.

LEFT, Herb soufflé; RIGHT, Turbot gratin

COLD CHICKEN PIE

SERVES 8

2 large chickens, roasting or boiling fowls
1 onion, peeled and halved
1 carrot, halved
1 stalk celery
1 bay leaf
3 stalks parsley
sea salt
whole black peppercorns
1 packet (15 g/½ oz) gelatine

Pastry:
250 g (9 oz) plain flour, sifted
pinch of salt
75 g (3 oz) butter, diced
50 g (2 oz) lard, diced
1 egg
4–5 tablespoons iced water

beaten egg yolk, to glaze

Preparation time: 45 minutes, plus cooling and chilling
Cooking time: 2¼–4 hours
Oven: 180°C, 350°F, Gas Mark 4

Although this pie is best eaten the day after baking, it can be kept perfectly well for up to one week in the refrigerator. It makes an excellent cold main course, needing as accompaniments only chutneys and a salad or two.

1. Put the two birds with the flavouring vegetables and herbs, some salt and black peppercorns in a large pan, and cover with water. (Use hot water for roasting birds, cold water for boiling fowls.) Bring to the boil, cover the pan, and simmer 1¼ hours for roasting chickens and 3 hours for boilers. If you do not have a large enough pan, cook the birds one after the other in the same stock. If you use a pressure cooker, reduce the cooking time by two-thirds. When the time is up, lift out the birds and leave to cool, throw away the vegetables and herbs, and strain the stock.

2. While the birds are cooking, make the pastry. Put the sifted flour and salt in a bowl, add the butter and lard and rub into the flour with the fingertips. Mix in the egg. Add the iced water gradually, mixing until the dough gathers into a ball. Turn out and wrap in cling film, then chill for 2 hours low down in the refrigerator.

3. Cut the meat off the carcasses, discarding all skin, and divide it into neat fillets. Put 1 teaspoon sea salt and 6 black peppercorns in a mortar and crush roughly. Roll out two-thirds of the pastry until just under 1 cm (½ inch) thick, and use it to line a greased hinged pie mould or an 18 cm (7 inch) round cake tin with a removable base.

4. Make layers of chicken in the pastry case, sprinkling each layer with crushed sea salt and black pepper. Add 4 tablespoons of the strained chicken stock, having removed the fat, and cover with a pastry lid.

5. Seal the edges by damping them, then pinching together and rolling to form a rim. Make a decorative centrepiece from the trimmings, and stick in the middle of the pie. Cut round it with a sharp knife so that it can be removed after baking. Brush all over with beaten egg yolk, put in a preheated oven and bake for 1 hour.

6. While the pie is cooking measure the stock and allow 1 packet (15 g/½ oz) gelatine to each 600 ml (1 pint). Dissolve the gelatine in a little of the heated stock, then mix it with the rest of the cold liquid.

7. After baking, remove the centrepiece while the pie is still hot and pour the cool stock in through a funnel. Do this very slowly, waiting for it to settle before adding more, until the pie is full up. Leave to cool completely, replace the centrepiece, and keep in the refrigerator until required.

Variation: For Cold game pie substitute 450 g (1 lb) stewing venison, 450 g (1 lb) rabbit, jointed, and 1 pheasant or 2 partridges for the chicken, and cook the meats with the flavouring vegetables and herbs for 2 hours, or 40 minutes under pressure. Then proceed as for the Cold chicken pie, making alternate layers of venison cut in small pieces, pieces of rabbit, and fillets of game. Crush 1 teaspoon sea salt, 8 black peppercorns, and 8 juniper berries roughly in a mortar and sprinkle over each layer. Bake as for Cold chicken pie.

ROAST GOOSE WITH CELERY STUFFING

SERVES 6–8

1 goose, about 6 kg (13 lb)

Stuffing:
1 head celery
250 g (9 oz) slightly stale white bread, crusts removed, and made into breadcrumbs
½ tablespoon sea salt
1 teaspoon black peppercorns, crushed
¼ teaspoon ground mace
2 eggs, beaten
50 g (2 oz) butter, semi-melted

Preparation time: 25 minutes
Cooking time: 5–5½ hours
Oven: 200°C, 400°F, Gas Mark 6; then 180°C, 350°F, Gas Mark 4

I find the best way to roast a goose is without any stuffing at all, since this allows the excess fat to drain away freely. This is rarely possible, however, as the goose does not feed many, and usually requires a stuffing to make the meat go further. A compromise, although tricky to do, is to stuff the bird after the first 20 minutes, by which time quite a lot of fat has already drained off. Alternatively, it can be simply stuffed with unpeeled quartered apples, which add a tart flavour to the flesh. This stuffing is not eaten, but left in the bird.

1. Remove the giblets from the bird and set aside for stock. Weigh the goose before stuffing it in order to calculate the cooking time. Allow 25 minutes per lb, unstuffed weight.
2. Make the stuffing. Discard the outer stalks of the celery, trim the rest and chop finely. Put in a bowl with the breadcrumbs, salt, peppercorns and mace. Stir in the eggs and butter and mix well.
3. Prick the surface of the bird all over with a skewer, and place upside down on a rack in a roasting tin. (Only turn the right way up for the last ½ hour, but do not baste at any stage.) Place in a preheated moderately hot oven and cook for 20 minutes.

4. Remove the bird from the oven, stuff it with the celery stuffing and return to the oven, having reduced the heat to moderate.
5. While the bird is cooking, make stock with the giblets in the usual way, i.e. simmer them in a pan with half an onion and water to cover generously for about an hour.
6. When it is cooked, transfer the bird to a hot platter and keep warm. Pour the pan juices into a bowl and stand for a few minutes to allow the fat to rise to the top. Separate the juices from the fat. Place the roasting tin over a low flame and scrape all the residues together, adding the fat-free pan juices, and the giblet stock. Stir all together and pour into a small jug to serve with the goose.
7. The roast goose may be accompanied by an apple sauce, the traditional sauce for goose. A recipe for Apple sauce is given below.

APPLE SAUCE

SERVES 4–6
2 large cooking apples, peeled and cored
3 tablespoons water
½ teaspoon sugar
2 teaspoons lemon juice
15 g (½ oz) butter

Preparation time: 10 minutes, plus cooling
Cooking time: 8–10 minutes

This sauce, which may be served either hot or cold, is excellent with roast goose, duck or pork.
1. Slice the apples, and put in a small pan with the water and sugar. Bring to the boil, cover, and simmer gently until soft, stirring often to prevent sticking. Cool slightly.
2. Process the apple briefly in a food processor, stopping before it is completely smooth. Alternatively, push the apple through a sieve or even simply mash it

with a potato masher if you prefer a rougher sauce. Add the lemon juice and butter and mix well. Tip into a sauce boat and serve.

TOP, Apple sauce; BOTTOM, Roast goose with celery stuffing

ROAST VENISON

SERVES 6
Marinade:
4 tablespoons olive oil
1 medium onion, peeled
1 large carrot, sliced
2 stalks celery, sliced
1 clove garlic, peeled and chopped
3 stalks parsley, chopped
1 bay leaf, crumbled
6 black peppercorns
6 juniper berries
½ teaspoon sea salt
350 ml (12 fl oz) red wine
a saddle or haunch of venison weighing
about 1.5–2 kg (3½–4½ lb)

To cook the meat:
10 black peppercorns
10 juniper berries
1 clove garlic, chopped
50 g (2 oz) butter, at room temperature
a little wine or boiling water

Preparation time: 20 minutes, plus
marinating for 2 days and standing
Cooking time: 1 hour 40 minutes–2 hours
Oven: 200°C, 400°F, Gas Mark 6; then
180°C, 350°F, Gas Mark 4

This wonderfully festive dish, evocative of Dickensian Christmases at their richest, needs some advance preparation. To bring out the flavours fully the venison should ideally be marinated for two days before cooking.

1. Prepare the marinade: Heat the oil and cook the vegetables gently for 5 minutes. Add the parsley, bay leaf, peppercorns and juniper berries which you have crushed roughly in a mortar with the sea salt. Add the wine, bring to the boil, and simmer for 20 minutes. Leave to cool before using. (For a large joint, double the quantities.)

2. 24–48 hours before you plan to cook the venison, weigh it to calculate the cooking time, then pour the marinade over it and leave in a cool place, basting from time to time.

3. When ready to cook the joint lift it out of the marinade and pat it dry. Crush the fresh peppercorns and juniper berries roughly in a mortar with the chopped garlic. Rub the meat all over with the butter, then coat with the crushed seasonings.

4. Stand the venison on a rack in a roasting tin and cook for 30 minutes in a preheated moderately hot oven, basting with the butter.

5. Strain the marinade and boil it up until it has reduced to 150 ml (¼ pint) for a small to medium joint, or 300 ml (½ pint) for a large one.

6. When the 30 minutes are up, reduce the oven to moderate and pour the marinade over the meat. Allow 20 minutes per 450 g (1 lb) cooking time in all for joints weighing up to 1.5 kg (3½ lb), and 15 minutes per 450 g (1 lb) for large joints. This should give a medium rare result; if you prefer your venison to be very rare, decrease the time accordingly.

7. When the cooking time is up, lift the venison on to a heated platter and stand for 10 minutes before carving.

8. Add a drop of wine (or boiling water) to the juices in the roasting tin, and scrape all together for a moment or two over a moderate heat. Pour into a small jug and serve with the meat. Venison is also very good when accompanied by redcurrant or crab-apple jelly, or Cranberry sauce (see page 19), and a purée of potatoes, Brussels sprouts, carrots, and braised celery. Serve all this together for a truly festive meal.

CARBONADE FLAMANDE

SERVES 6

1.25 kg (2½ lb) best stewing steak cut in thick
   slices
450 ml (¾ pint) lager
1 bay leaf
40 g (1½ oz) butter
1 tablespoon olive oil
2 large onions, peeled and coarsely chopped
2 large garlic cloves, peeled and finely
   chopped
1½ tablespoons tomato purée
1½ tablespoons plain flour
sea salt
freshly ground black pepper

To garnish:
3 slices dry white bread
2–3 tablespoons Dijon mustard

Preparation time: 25 minutes
Cooking time: 2 hours 15 minutes – 4
hours 15 minutes
Oven: 180°C, 350°F, Gas Mark 4

This is a casserole of beef stewed in beer, garnished with slices of dry bread spread with Dijon mustard. It is simple to make, and eminently suitable for the days between Christmas and the New Year, needing only a potato purée and green salad to turn it into a very satisfying meal.
1. Cut the sliced beef into rectangles about 4 cm (1½ inch) square. Put them in a flameproof casserole and pour the lager over them. Add the bay leaf and bring to the boil on top of the stove. Once boiling point is reached, cover the casserole and transfer it to a preheated oven. Allow 2 hours cooking time for best stewing steak; for a cheaper cut, allow 3–4 hours in a cooler oven.
2. Heat the butter and oil in a large frying pan and cook the onions slowly, stirring often, until they are light golden. Add the garlic halfway through. When both are lightly browned, add the tomato purée, then the flour, stirring till blended.

Simmer gently for 2 minutes, stirring almost continuously, then remove from the heat.
3. Thirty minutes before the beef cooking time is up, take the crusts off the garnish bread, and cut each slice into 4 triangles. Dry them in the bottom of the oven, until crisp and lightly coloured.
4. When the beef is ready, transfer it to the top of the stove. Drop in the onion mixture by degrees, stirring until each addition is amalgamated. Simmer gently for 5 minutes, stirring now and then, and adding salt and pepper to taste.
5. To serve, tip the contents of the casserole into a serving dish. Spread the triangles of dried bread with Dijon mustard and lay them on top of the stew, or around the edges of the dish.

GRILLED LEG OF LAMB

1 small leg of English lamb
4 tablespoons best olive oil
juice of 1 lemon
a few sprigs fresh rosemary, marjoram and
   thyme
black pepper, coarsely ground

Preparation time: 10 minutes, plus
marinating
Cooking time: about 30 minutes

This is an excellent dish which I used to cook over the fire in a cottage in the country. I now make it under the grill, and it is as good as ever; better in a way, for there is less shrinkage. Ask your butcher to 'butterfly' the lamb for you: in other words, to open it out flat, after boning, so that you get a roughly rectangular piece of meat, more or less even in thickness. Lamb cooked this way is just as good eaten cold as hot, well worth cooking specially a day beforehand. Otherwise, keep any remains from the hot joint in a cold larder, not in the refrigerator, for serving the next day, with a cake of mashed potato and fried onion, and a salad.
1. Prepare the lamb 2–4 hours in advance. Rub it all over with olive oil, sprinkle with

lemon juice, and scatter fresh herbs and black pepper all over. Leave for a few hours before grilling.
2. Heat the grill to its highest point and lay the lamb on the rack, skin side up. Grill for about 15 minutes on each side, depending on how you like your lamb cooked. Keep it on the pink side, for it will go on cooking for a bit after you remove it from the grill. Stand, covered loosely with a sheet of foil, in a warm place for 10–15 minutes.
3. Lay the lamb on a board to carve, in neat slices about 7 mm (⅓ inch) thick. Be careful to catch the juices that run out. Serve with a potato purée, or a purée of root vegetables (see page 15), a green salad, and a fruit jelly: crab-apple, red-currant, or medlar.

TOP, Carbonade flamande; BOTTOM, Grilled leg of lamb

TORTELLINI (OR RAVIOLI) ALLA PANNA

Filling:
225 g (8 oz) spinach, washed and drained
350 g (12 oz) ricotta
1 egg yolk
50 g (2 oz) grated Parmesan
freshly grated nutmeg
sea salt
freshly ground black pepper

Pasta:
2 whole eggs plus 2 egg whites
4 teaspoons olive oil
2 teaspoons water
a pinch of sea salt
350 g (12 oz) plain flour

Sauce:
50 g (2 oz) butter
300 ml (½ pint) single cream
salt
freshly ground black pepper
50–75 g (2–3 oz) freshly grated Parmesan

Preparation time: about 60 minutes, plus cooling and chilling
Cooking time: about 30 minutes

Tortellini filled with spinach and ricotta are traditionally eaten on Christmas Eve in northern Italy, since no meat may be eaten until after Midnight Mass. Tortellini are very fiddly to make by hand, unless you are an accomplished pasta maker, so I suggest making ravioli instead, or buying tortellini already made (the method for both is the same until you reach the cutting or shaping stage): you will need 750 g (1¾ lb), but be sure they don't have a meat filling for this will not go with the cream sauce.

1. First make the filling. Drop the spinach into a pan of lightly salted boiling water and cook for 5 minutes, then drain in a colander. When the spinach is cool enough to handle, squeeze out any excess moisture and chop it roughly by hand.

2. Put the spinach in a food processor with the ricotta, egg yolk, Parmesan, nutmeg, salt and pepper. Process to a smooth paste, turn into a bowl, and chill for at least 30 minutes.

3. Then make the dough. If using a regular-sized food processor, this is best done in two parts. Put 1 egg and 1 white in the processor with 2 teaspoons olive oil, 1 teaspoon water, and a pinch of salt. Process for 30 seconds, then add 175 g (6 oz) flour and process for another 30 seconds. Form into a ball, wrap in floured cling film, and rest for 5 minutes while you repeat the process with the rest of the ingredients.

4. Have the setting of your pasta mill set at the broadest setting. Flatten one half of the dough with the heel of your hand, and feed it through the rollers. Fold the resulting strip in three, and feed it through again. Do this three times, then start to move the rollers one notch closer, feeding it through once each time, until you reach the finest setting bar one. Stop there, and cover the strips with a damp cloth while you repeat the process with the remainder of the dough. When both lots of dough are rolled out, you can start making the pasta shapes.

5. There are various ways of making ravioli. Some people use a metal tray, others use a metal cutter like a biscuit cutter, or a special rolling pin. Make the ravioli according to your equipment, filling each one with about ½ teaspoon of the filling.

6. When all are made, bring a broad pan of lightly salted water to the boil. When the water boils, drop in the ravioli, a few at a time so that they can float freely. Cook for 2 minutes, if freshly made; if made a day in advance, allow 3 minutes. (If using bought tortellini, allow 4–5 minutes cooking, testing carefully, then treat like ravioli.)

7. While the ravioli or tortellini are cooking, put the butter and cream for the sauce in a pan with salt and pepper to taste, and warm gently without allowing the mixture to come to the boil.

8. Once the ravioli or tortellini are ready, drain them in a colander while the next batch are cooking, then tip them all into a heated bowl. Pour some of the cream sauce over them, and sprinkle them with the grated Parmesan, keeping some back for the garnish. Mix the pasta, sauce and Parmesan together gently and tip them into a clean serving dish, scattering the remaining Parmesan over the top. Serve as soon as possible.

Tortellini alla panna

SPINACH ROULADE WITH PEPPER SAUCE

Filling:
225 g (8 oz) curd cheese, quark, or ricotta
2 tablespoons yogurt
sea salt
freshly ground black pepper
2 tablespoons chopped spring onions
2 tablespoons chopped fresh tarragon, or parsley

Pepper sauce:
1 small onion, peeled and finely chopped
25 g (1 oz) butter
1 tablespoon olive oil
450 g (1 lb) tomatoes, skinned and chopped
2 red peppers, skinned, seeded and chopped
½ bay leaf
sea salt
freshly ground black pepper
a pinch of sugar
1 tablespoon finely chopped fresh coriander

Roulade:
750 g (1½ lb) fresh spinach, washed and drained
3 tablespoons double cream
1 teaspoon sea salt
freshly ground black pepper
5 large eggs, separated
3 tablespoons grated Parmesan

To garnish:
fresh chives
sprigs fresh tarragon

Preparation time: 40 minutes, plus cooling
Cooking time: about 30 minutes
Oven: 200°C, 400°F, Gas Mark 6

This makes a good main course for a vegetarian meal, or a first course before a very simple main dish, like a cold grilled leg of lamb, when it will serve 6. The tomatoes and peppers in the sauce are best skinned over an open flame or under a grill, which gives them a lovely smokey flavour.

1. To make the filling, beat the curd cheese (quark, or ricotta) together with the yogurt, adding salt and pepper to taste. Stir in the spring onions and herb and set aside.

2. To make the sauce, cook the onion gently in the butter and oil for 5 minutes, then add the tomatoes and continue to cook gently for 5 minutes. Add the peppers and cook for another 5 minutes, followed by the bay leaf, salt and pepper, and sugar.

3. Cool for a little, then purée briefly in a food processor or blender. Tip into a small pan and stir in the chopped coriander. Leave until the last minute to reheat.

4. For the roulade, first line a 30 × 20 × 2 cm (12 × 8 × ¾ inch) Swiss roll tin with non-stick silicone paper. Throw the spinach in lightly salted boiling water, cook for 5 minutes, then drain well and leave to cool.

5. When the spinach is cool enough to handle, squeeze out excess moisture, and chop roughly, by hand. Put the spinach in a bowl and add the cream, with salt and pepper to taste. Then stir in the lightly beaten egg yolks. Beat the whites until stiff, and fold into the spinach mixture.

6. Spread the mixture into the prepared tin, and scatter the grated Parmesan over the top. Bake in a preheated oven for 10–12 minutes, or until firm.

7. Remove from the oven and turn the tin upside down over another sheet of non-stick silicone paper. Turn out the roulade, remove the tin, and carefully peel off the first sheet of paper. Spread the filling over the roulade, then roll it up gently, using the second piece of paper as an aid. Slide on to a heated dish and serve as soon as possible, garnished with chives and tarragon and with the reheated pepper sauce in a separate bowl.

SAUERKRAUT WITH FRANKFURTERS

SERVES 6–8
1.25–1.5 kg (2½–3 lb) sauerkraut
75 g (3 oz) butter
1 large onion, peeled and chopped
4 rashers streaky bacon, cut in strips
10 juniper berries, or ½ teaspoon caraway
   seeds
2 tablespoons sea salt
10 black peppercorns
2 teaspoons sugar
8 pairs large Frankfurters
2 medium potatoes, peeled and coarsely
   grated
300 ml (½ pint) soured cream

Preparation time: 20 minutes
Cooking time: 2 hours 20 minutes
Oven: 150°C, 300°F, Gas Mark 2

This is a hearty dish such as you might find in Alsace, or in a Parisian brasserie. It is just the thing for lunch on a cold winter's day. Sauerkraut can be bought, usually in tins from Poland or Czechoslovakia, in many delicatessens.
1. Rinse the sauerkraut briefly under the cold tap, breaking it up with the fingers.
2. Melt the butter in a heavy flameproof casserole and cook the onion till it starts to turn golden. Then add the strips of bacon, and cook until they have coloured. Tip in the sauerkraut and stir until it is well mixed with the onion.
3. Add enough cold water to come barely level with the sauerkraut, adding the juniper berries or caraway seeds, sea salt, peppercorns, and sugar.
4. Bring to the boil, cover, transfer to a preheated oven and cook for 2 hours.

5. Just before the 2 hours are up, drop the Frankfurters into a large pan of very hot water – keep it just below boiling point – and leave them for 8 minutes, then turn off the heat and leave them in the water until ready to serve.
6. When the sauerkraut is ready, transfer it to the top of the stove, over a low heat. Stir in the grated potato and cook gently, stirring often, for 10 minutes. Then stir in the sour cream and adjust the seasoning.
7. To serve, pile the sauerkraut on a large platter and lay the drained sausages on it. The only accompaniments this dish calls for are some plain boiled potatoes and a good mustard.

EGGS IN MACARONI CHEESE

175 g (6 oz) macaroni
6 eggs
40 g (1½ oz) butter
2 rounded tablespoons plain flour
600 ml (1 pint) milk, heated
150 ml (¼ pint) single cream
150 g (5 oz) Gruyère cheese, grated
6 thin slices ham

Preparation time: 25 minutes, plus cooling
Cooking time: about 30 minutes
Oven (optional): 200°C, 400°F, Gas Mark 6

1. Cook the macaroni in plenty of boiling, lightly salted water, drain and set aside.
2. Put the eggs in boiling water and boil for five minutes exactly, then cool and shell them.
3. Melt the butter, stir in the flour and blend with the heated milk. Add the cream and 100 g (4 oz) of the grated cheese. Mix with the macaroni.
4. Wrap each egg carefully in a slice of ham. Pour a thin layer of the macaroni into a shallow dish, lay the eggs-in-ham on it, and cover with the rest of the macaroni.
5. Sprinkle with the remaining cheese and cook in a preheated oven for about 15 minutes, or until golden brown on top and re-heated all through. Alternatively, if everything has been kept hot, the dish may simply be browned under the grill.
6. Serve hot with a lettuce salad.

TOP, Sauerkraut with frankfurters; BOTTOM, Eggs in macaroni cheese

BAKED GLAZED HAM

SERVES 10–12
1 ham or gammon, 3.5–4.5 kg/8–10 lb
3 large onions
4 stalks celery
3 large carrots
2 turnips
2 parsnips
4 stalks parsley
2 bay leaves
15 peppercorns
225 g (8 oz) granulated sugar
300 ml (½ pint) cider vinegar
1 cup soft brown sugar
½ cup fresh brown breadcrumbs
1 dessertspoon French mustard
1 tablespoon cider vinegar

Preparation time: 15 minutes, plus cooling
Cooking time: 3 hours – 4 hours 5 minutes
Oven: 180°C, 350°F, Gas Mark 4

1. Soak the ham in cold water for 24 hours then remove from the water and put in a large saucepan with the vegetables, parsley, herbs, vinegar and granulated sugar. Cover with cold water and bring almost to boiling point.
2. Time the cooking from the first moment bubbles start to reach the surface. Do not allow it ever to reach simmering, far less boiling, point. Allow 20 minutes per 450 g (1 lb), skimming off any brown froth that rises to the surface. Keep the heat well below boiling point all the time.
3. When the cooking time is up, turn off the heat, pour in a cup of cold water to arrest the cooking, and leave the ham to cool in the water. When cool, lift the ham out of the water and remove the skin.
4. Mix the brown sugar and breadcrumbs to a paste with the mustard and vinegar. Smooth the mixture all over the fatty surface of the ham with a palette knife, pressing well in. Do not do this too far in advance of the baking or most of it will slide off.
5. Bake for 45 minutes in a preheated oven, basting half-way through with a little extra vinegar. Leave for 15 minutes in the oven with the heat turned off and the door slightly open, or in a warm place before attempting to carve. Serve with Cumberland sauce or mustard sauce.

TOP, Glazed baked ham; BOTTOM, Jambon persillé

JAMBON PERSILLÉ

SERVES 12
½ ham or gammon, about 2.75 kg (6 lb)
450 g (1 lb) knuckle of veal
4 calves' feet, or pigs' feet if calves' feet are unobtainable
1 bay leaf
2 stalks parsley
1 stalk celery
10 shallots, or 6 small onions, peeled
2 cloves
12 black peppercorns
2 bottles dry white wine
3 tablespoons white wine vinegar
4 tablespoons chopped parsley

Preparation time: 45 minutes, plus soaking for 24 hours and cooling overnight
Cooking time: 3½ hours

1. Soak the ham or gammon for 24 hours, changing the water two or three times. Put it in a large pot and cover with fresh cold water. Bring to the boil and simmer for 30 minutes. Leave it to cool, then cut out the bone. Reserve the water.
2. Blanch in a similar fashion the knuckle of veal and the calves' (or pigs') feet, but only for 10 minutes. Drain and rinse well under running water.
3. Clean the large pot and put in the ham, veal, and feet, the herbs, celery, shallots, cloves and peppercorns – no salt is needed. Pour over the white wine, add enough of the reserved blanching water (from the ham if it is not too salty, otherwise from the veal etc) to cover the meat. Bring to the boil, removing all scum with a slotted spoon as it rises to the surface, and simmer very gently with the lid on the pot for 3 hours.
4. Take out the ham, throw away the veal, calves' feet and the flavouring vegetables and herbs, and strain the liquid. Cut the ham in fairly large pieces, about 2.5–5 cm (1–2 inch) cubes, and crush slightly with a fork. Press the pieces into a round bowl, such as a shallow pudding basin, mixing the fat and lean evenly. Now mix the white wine vinegar and the chopped parsley into the bowl, ensuring that the parsley is spread evenly amongst the ham pieces.
5. Strain the liquid again through a double muslin and remove all the fat. Pour it over the ham, making sure it penetrates all through the pieces and reaches the bottom of the bowl. Leave to cool overnight, in the refrigerator or a cool larder.
6. To serve, turn out on to a flat platter and cut in slices.

HERB-STUFFED VINE LEAVES

150 ml (¼ pint) olive oil
225 g (8 oz) onions, peeled and chopped
100 g (4 oz) Italian medium-grain rice,
    washed and drained
600 ml (1 pint) boiling water
2 tablespoons pine kernels
2 tablespoons seedless raisins
sea salt
freshly ground black pepper
3 tablespoons lemon juice
3 tablespoons chopped fresh mixed herbs: dill,
    tarragon and parsley
225 g (8 oz) preserved vine leaves or 24 fresh
    vine leaves

Preparation time: 35 minutes, plus
cooling
Cooking time: about 1 hour

1. Heat half the oil in a frying pan and cook the onion until softened and pale golden. Add the rice to the pan. Stir around for 2–3 minutes. Pour on 300 ml (½ pint) boiling water. Add the pine kernels and the raisins, and salt and pepper to taste. Simmer gently until the water is absorbed, about 8–10 minutes. Add more salt and pepper if needed, 1 tablespoon lemon juice and the chopped herbs.
2. Turn out on to a plate to cool while you prepare the vine leaves. (These can be bought in packets or cans from Greek and Cypriot shops.) Soak them in a sink full of cold water for a minute or two, then gently separate them and lay on a wire rack to drain. If using fresh vine leaves, blanch them for 3 minutes in boiling water, then drain.
3. When the stuffing has cooled, place a heaped tablespoon in the centre of each leaf, then roll it up loosely into a cigar shape, leaving room for the rice to swell.
4. Put a layer of unused leaves in the bottom of a broad pan and lay the filled leaves on them. Pour over the remaining olive oil, 2 tablespoons lemon juice, and 300 ml (½ pint) hot water. Lay a flat plate on top of the vine leaves to press them down lightly, and cover the pan. Bring to the boil and simmer gently for 45 minutes. Leave to cool in the pan.
5. To serve, lay the little rolls on a flat dish and sprinkle with a little more lemon juice. Serve as a first course, or with cocktails.

SPAGHETTI WITH QUICK CLAM SAUCE

40 g (1½ oz) butter
1 shallot or small onion, peeled and chopped
1 clove garlic, peeled and crushed
1 × 225 g (8 oz) can minced clams
150 ml (¼ pint) white wine, or clam juice
450 g (1 lb) spaghetti
150 ml (¼ pint) double cream
freshly ground black pepper
2 tablespoons chopped parsley

Preparation time: 15 minutes
Cooking time: 15–25 minutes

LEFT, Herb-stuffed vine leaves; BOTTOM, Spaghetti with quick clam sauce

1. Melt the butter and cook the shallot or onion in it until it is a pale golden colour. Add the garlic and cook for a few moments longer.
2. Open the tin of clams, drain the liquid into the pan and add the wine or clam juice. Simmer gently for 8 minutes.
3. Meanwhile, cook the spaghetti in plenty of boiling, lightly salted water until tender.
4. Stir the cream into the sauce, reheat and add pepper to taste. Add the minced clams and reheat without allowing the mixture to boil. Add the parsley and keep warm while the spaghetti is cooking. Drain well, pour the sauce over and serve.

VEGETARIAN CASSEROLE

100–150 g (4–5 oz) buckwheat or couscous
2 tablespoons oil
25 g (1 oz) butter
1 large onion, peeled and sliced
2 leeks, cleaned and sliced
2 carrots, sliced
3 courgettes, chopped
225 g (8 oz) tomatoes, peeled and thickly
    sliced
salt
freshly ground black pepper
1 egg
1 tablespoon plain flour
300 ml (½ pint) yogurt

Preparation time: 25–30 minutes
Cooking time: 30 minutes, plus cooking buckwheat
Oven: 180°C, 350°F, Gas Mark 4

1. Cook the buckwheat or couscous according to the directions on the packet. Put the cooked buckwheat or couscous in the bottom of a buttered casserole.
2. Heat the oil and butter in a frying pan, add the onion and leeks and cook until soft and lightly coloured.
3. Parboil the carrots until almost tender; drain, reserving the cooking water. Add the unpeeled courgettes to the onion and leeks; cover the pan and simmer gently for 4 minutes, then add the sliced carrots and a little of their cooking water. Stew gently for another 3–4 minutes.
4. Add the tomatoes and cook very briefly. Season the vegetables well with salt and pepper and pour over the grain in the casserole.
5. Beat the egg, stir in the flour and beat into the yogurt. Add salt and pepper to taste and pour the mixture over the vegetables. Cover the casserole and cook in a preheated oven for 30 minutes.
6. Serve the casserole with a green salad.

GARLIC OMELETTE

SERVES 2
2 slices dry bread
50 g (2 oz) butter
1 large clove garlic, peeled and crushed
5 eggs
sea salt
freshly ground black pepper
½ tablespoon finely chopped parsley

Preparation time: 10 minutes
Cooking time: 8–10 minutes

This omelette will serve 2 people. Large omelettes are awkward to make: it is better to prepare 2 smaller ones if you are cooking for 4 people.
1. Trim the crusts off the bread, and cut each slice into small cubes. Heat most of the butter in a frying pan, leaving just enough to cook the omelette. Fry the bread until golden, stirring constantly and add the crushed garlic. Remove from the pan and drain on absorbent kitchen paper. Set aside.
2. Break the eggs into a bowl. Beat lightly with a fork and season with salt and pepper. Heat the remaining butter in an omelette pan and pour in the eggs. As the eggs start to set, tip in the garlic-flavoured croutons and continue to cook quickly, turning the omelette out on to a warmed flat dish before the eggs have completely set. Sprinkle with chopped parsley and serve immediately.

TOP, Vegetarian casserole; BOTTOM, Garlic omelette

SMALL MUTTON PIES

MAKES 12 SMALL PIES
1 kg (2 lb) pastry, short, flaky or puff
1 kg (2 lb) minced leg of lamb, with the bone,
  if possible
2 onions, peeled
2 carrots, scrubbed
1 stalk celery
½ bay leaf
2 tablespoons chopped parsley
sea salt
freshly ground black pepper
1 egg yolk

Preparation time: 45 minutes, plus
cooling
Cooking time: 45 minutes
Oven: 200°C, 400°F, Gas Mark 6

These pies are excellent hot, cold, or re-heated. They will also keep hot for hours without spoiling. We always used to have them for picnics when we lived in Scotland.
1. When buying the minced lamb, ask the butcher for a bone as well. In the morning of your cooking day, make about a pint of stock with the bone, 1 carrot, 1 onion, the stalk celery and the half bay leaf simmered in water. (Alternatively, use beef stock or a cube.) Strain the stock, leave to cool, then remove the fat.
2. Later in the day, make the meat filling. Chop the remaining onion and carrot finely and mix with the meat and the chopped parsley. Put in a saucepan with 450 ml (¾ pint) of the stock and bring to the boil. Add salt and pepper to taste and simmer gently, stirring often, for 10 minutes. Turn into a colander over a bowl and leave to cool.

3. When the filling in the colander has cooled completely, roll out the pastry very thin indeed. Line 12 small round tins (about 7.5 cm/3 inch across and 3 cm/1¼ inch deep) with pastry and divide the filling among them. Pour 2 tablespoons of the cooking liquid into each pie and cover with a pastry lid. Brush with beaten egg yolk and make a small slit in the centre of each pie.
4. Bake in a preheated oven for 25–35 minutes, according to size, watching to make sure they do not burn.
5. Remove the pies from the oven and using a funnel pour the remaining 150 ml (¼ pint) of stock into each one. (If you prefer, the stock can be slightly thickened first, with 1 teaspoon of flour mixed with 1 teaspoon of butter.) This step can be omitted entirely, but it does ensure that the pies are not dry.

BRAISED PHEASANT

SERVES 3–4
40 g (1½ oz) beef dripping, bacon fat or
  butter
1 carrot, chopped
1 onion, peeled and chopped
1 leek, chopped
1 stalk celery, chopped
1 oven-ready pheasant
300 ml (½ pint) stock
150 ml (¼ pint) red wine
1 teaspoon plain flour
150 ml (¼ pint) sour cream
sea salt
freshly ground black pepper

Preparation time: about 25 minutes
Cooking time: 1 hour 20 minutes
Oven: 160°C, 300°F, Gas Mark 2

A young or roasting pheasant is best for this recipe.
1. Heat the fat in a heavy flameproof casserole and add the chopped vegetables; cook them gently, stirring, for 2–3 minutes. Push to the sides of the pan, put in the pheasant and brown on all sides.
2. Heat the stock with the wine and pour on to the bird. Add salt and pepper, cover the casserole and cook in a preheated oven. For well-done pheasant, allow 1 hour. Baste and turn the bird from one side to the other now and then.
3. When done, remove the pheasant from the oven and carve. Lift out the vegetables with a slotted spoon and put them into a serving dish; lay the carved birds over them. Reserve the liquor.

4. Keep the dish warm while you make the sauce: mix the flour into the sour cream in a saucepan. Measure 150 ml (¼ pint) of the cooking liquor and strain into the saucepan. Stir over gentle heat until slightly thickened and smooth. Serve in a sauceboat, with the game, or pour it over if you prefer.

TOP, Small mutton pies; BOTTOM, Braised pheasant

DRIED FRUIT SALAD

SERVES 4–5

225 g (8 oz) mixed dried fruit: apples, pears,
    apricots, peaches, prunes, figs
2 tablespoons raisins
½ teaspoon grated orange rind
½ teaspoon grated lemon rind
2 tablespoons sugar
juice of 1 orange
2 tablespoons coarsely chopped almonds

Preparation time: 15–20 minutes plus
soaking and cooling
Cooking time: about 15 minutes

1. Soak the fruit if necessary. Cover with cold water (or the water they were soaked in) and cook fairly quickly until soft, but not disintegrated. The timing varies widely according to the fruit; soaked fruit of good quality should take about 15 minutes.
2. At the end of the cooking, add the raisins, the grated rind and the sugar. Leave to cool, then stir in the orange juice and the chopped nuts.
3. If there is too much juice after cooking, do not stir in the orange juice, and use a slotted spoon to remove the fruit to a serving dish with the chopped almonds stirred in. Boil the juice to the desired amount, then pour over the fruit and nuts.

Pour over the orange juice as well.
4. Serve while still warm, or completely cool, but do not chill. Serve with a bowl of cream.

BAKED APPLE DUMPLINGS

SERVES 6
Short pastry:
350 g (12 oz) plain flour
a pinch of salt
½ teaspoon sugar
175 g (6 oz) butter
1 egg yolk
a little lemon juice
a little water
2 tablespoons raisins
1 tablespoon brandy
6 eating apples, e.g. Granny Smith's or
    Coxes, peeled and cored
2 tablespoons soft brown sugar
40 g (1½ oz) butter
1 egg yolk, beaten
caster sugar

Preparation time: 35 minutes
Cooking time: 40 minutes
Oven: 200°C, 400°F, Gas Mark 6; then
180°C, 350°F, Gas Mark 4

1. Make the pastry: sift the flour and salt into a bowl. Add the sugar and rub in the butter, using the fingertips, until the mixture resembles fine breadcrumbs. Add the egg yolk and lemon juice and sufficient water to mix into a pliable dough. Knead lightly and chill for 1 hour before using.
2. Divide the pastry into 6 equal pieces and roll each one out to a very thin circle. Soak the raisins in the brandy and put 1 teaspoon in the cavity of each apple. Add 1 teaspoon soft brown sugar to each one and top with a knob of butter.

3. Lay a filled apple in the centre of each circle of pastry and trim off four pieces to make a shape roughly like a Maltese cross. Gather the four sides up and seal with beaten yolk of egg.
4. Bake the apple dumplings in a preheated moderately hot oven for 20 minutes, then turn the oven down to moderate and cook for a further 20 minutes.
5. Sprinkle with caster sugar and serve with lightly whipped cream.

TOP, Dried fruit salad; BOTTOM, Baked apple dumplings

BLAZING APPLES

450 ml (¾ pint) water
100 g (4 oz) sugar
6 apples, small Bramleys or eating apples,
*   e.g. Coxes or Granny Smith's, cored*
apricot jam, about half a jar
4 tablespoons rum

Preparation time: 20 minutes
Cooking time: about 30 minutes,
including reducing the syrup

This is a spectacular and delicious pudding; any remaining apples are also good eaten cold. If you have no rum, brandy or marc de Bourgogne can be used instead, or almost any liqueur for that matter.

1. Choose a broad pan with a lid, large enough to fit in all the apples in one layer – a sauté pan is ideal. Put the water and sugar in it and bring to the boil. Simmer until the sugar has dissolved and a thin syrup is formed.

2. Fill the cavities in the apples with apricot jam and lay them in the syrup. There will not be enough to cover them but this does not matter; they will cook in the steam. Cover the pan and cook gently for 8–10 minutes, or until the apples are tender, watching them like a hawk as they can very quickly collapse if left a minute too long. In fact, it is a good thing to have a couple of extra apples in reserve in case one or two do flop.

3. As soon as the apples are soft when pierced with a fine skewer, lift them out with a slotted spoon and lay them in a hot serving dish, again in one layer.

4. Keep them hot while you reduce the juice by fast boiling until it is thick and syrupy. It does not matter if some of the jam has become mixed with it. Pour it over the apples.

5. Just before serving, heat the rum gently in a small saucepan, light it, and pour over the apples. Serve while still flaming. Accompany with a jug of thick cream.

CINNAMON APPLE CHARLOTTE

1 kg (2 lb) cooking apples, peeled, cored and
*   sliced*
75 g (3 oz) sugar
1 tablespoon lemon juice
3 tablespoons water
50 g (2 oz) butter
3 slices slightly stale bread
50 g (2 oz) caster sugar
1 teaspoon cinnamon

Preparation time: 25 minutes
Cooking time: 25 minutes
Oven: 200°C, 400°F, Gas Mark 6

1. Stew the apples gently with the sugar, lemon juice and water in a covered pan till soft. Put them through the medium mesh of a food mill or through a sieve and keep hot in a shallow dish.

2. Melt the butter without allowing it to burn. Cut the crusts off the bread and cut each slice in quarters. Brush each side of the pieces with the melted butter and dip them in the sugar and cinnamon, which you have mixed together on a plate.

3. Lay the bread pieces on a greased baking sheet and cook in a preheated oven for 15 minutes, turning them over halfway through. Watch to see they do not burn; they should be a golden brown. Lay them on top of the apple purée and serve with thick cream.

TOP, Blazing apples; BOTTOM, Cinnamon apple charlotte

GINGERBREAD

MAKES 1 × 24 cm (9½ inch) SQUARE CAKE
275 g (10 oz) plain flour, sifted
1 teaspoon bicarbonate of soda
1 teaspoon baking powder
1½ teaspoons grated or ground ginger
½ teaspoon ground allspice
½ teaspoon ground cinnamon
½ teaspoon sea salt
2 eggs, beaten
6 tablespoons molasses or black treacle
6 tablespoons golden syrup
75 g (3 oz) soft dark brown sugar
175 g (6 oz) butter
150 ml (¼ pint) milk

Preparation time: about 25 minutes
Cooking time: 50 minutes
Oven: 180°C, 350°F, Gas Mark 4

1. Grease and line with greased grease-proof paper a cake tin, about 24 cm (9½ inches) square and 4 cm (1½ inch) deep.
2. Sift together into a bowl the flour, bicarbonate of soda, baking powder, spices and salt.
3. Add the eggs gradually, beating well.
4. Warm together the molasses (or treacle), syrup, sugar and butter until the butter and sugar have both melted, and pour the warm mixture into the flour and egg mixture.
5. Finally add the milk. (The mixture should be quite thin, of a pouring consistency. If not, add more milk.)
6. Pour into the prepared tin and bake in a preheated oven for 45 minutes.
7. Serve either warm, as a dessert with whipped cream, or after cooling completely, as a cake.

CUSTARD SAUCE

MAKES 300 ml (½ pint)
2 egg yolks
2 tablespoons home-made vanilla sugar, or plain caster sugar
300 ml (½ pint) milk
5 cm (2 inch) piece vanilla pod, if no vanilla sugar is available

Preparation time: 10 minutes, plus infusing vanilla pod if necessary
Cooking time: 10–15 minutes

A most excellent sauce, this bears no relation to commercial custard, and is a delicious accompaniment to almost all English puddings, either hot or cold. If you have no home-made vanilla sugar, heat the milk 20 minutes beforehand with a piece of vanilla pod in it. When just below boiling point, cover the pan and leave at the side of the stove for 20 minutes to allow the milk to infuse the flavour. Throw away the pod before mixing into the eggs.
1. Break the egg yolks into a bowl and beat with an electric beater or a wire whisk for 2 minutes, adding the vanilla sugar (or plain caster sugar) by degrees. When thick and creamy, heat the milk to boiling point and pour on, continuing to beat gently.
2. Return to the pan and stir constantly over a very gentle heat for a few minutes, until very slightly thickened. Remove from the heat immediately and keep warm over hot water.
3. If the custard is to be served cold, stir it often while cooling to prevent a skin forming.

Gingerbread, served with whipped cream

PRUNE MOUSSE

SERVES 4–5
225 g (8 oz) prunes
cold tea
50 g (2 oz) sugar
2 tablespoons brandy or 1 tablespoon lemon juice
300 ml (½ pint) double cream
3 egg whites

Preparation time: 25 minutes, plus soaking overnight and chilling
Cooking time: 20–30 minutes

1. Soak the prunes overnight in sufficient cold tea to cover them, then cook them very slowly in the tea, adding the sugar.
2. When soft, lift them out of the liquid and remove the stones. Put the flesh in a blender with enough of the juice to make a thick purée and blend.
3. Transfer the purée to a bowl or soufflé dish, and add the brandy or lemon juice to sharpen the flavour. Whip the cream until stiff but not dry, and fold in. Beat the egg whites stiffly and fold in.
4. Chill the mousse in the refrigerator for at least 2 hours before serving.

CASTLE PUDDINGS

3 eggs
75 g (3 oz) caster sugar
1 teaspoon grated lemon rind, or use vanilla sugar
75 g (3 oz) plain flour
75 g (3 oz) butter, semi-melted
shreds of lemon and lime peel, to decorate

Preparation time: 15 minutes
Cooking time: 20 minutes
Oven: 180°C, 350°F, Gas Mark 4

1. Lightly grease 4 dariole moulds.
2. Beat the eggs until very light and almost frothy, adding the sugar and lemon rind by degrees and beating continuously. Then shake in the flour, also by degrees, and lastly add the semi-melted butter.
3. When all is well mixed, pour it into the prepared moulds, put in a preheated oven and bake for 20 minutes.

4. Turn the puddings out of their moulds to serve, decorate with lemon and lime shreds and accompany with golden syrup heated with a little lemon juice, and a jug of cream.

TOP, Prune mousse; BOTTOM, Castle puddings

FRESH FRUIT SALAD

SERVES 6

4 kiwi fruit, skinned and thickly sliced
1 small Charentais or Ogen melon, skinned and cubed
4 red-skinned plums, cubed
225 g (8 oz) strawberries, halved
175 g (6 oz) green grapes, halved, and seeded

Juice:
1½ tablespoons caster sugar
juice of 2 oranges
juice of 2 limes

Preparation time: about 20 minutes plus chilling

This is just about my favourite dessert, especially when it comes at the end of a rich Christmas meal. I like to limit the colours to pink and greeny-white, and I cut the fruit up quite small.

1. Prepare the salad about 2 hours before serving, if possible. Cut each kiwi fruit slice into sections and quarter the strawberries, rather than halving, if they are large.
2. Mix all the fruit in a glass bowl, and scatter the sugar over them. Mix the juice of the oranges and limes and pour it over the fruit. Mix gently, then cover with cling film and chill for a couple of hours before serving.
3. Serve accompanied by cream if you like, although I prefer it with just the sharp flavours of the citrus fruit. Sweet biscuits like tuiles, or langues de chat are another possible accompaniment.

FRUIT AT CHRISTMAS
Fruit has always played a major part in the menus of Christmas, whether cooked in breads, pies and puddings, made the basis of warming and alcoholic drinks, or simply piled up in rich, colourful profusion as decorative centre-pieces on tables or sideboards. An old custom common to Christmas Eve in many parts of England was the wassailing of fruit trees. A steaming wassail bowl would be taken out to the orchard, cupfuls would be drunk and the dregs thrown over the trees as a way of urging them to bear a rich harvest in the coming year.

QUEEN OF PUDDINGS

300 ml (½ pint) milk
2 strips lemon peel
25 g (1 oz) unsalted butter
100 g (4 oz) caster sugar
50 g (2 oz) soft white breadcrumbs
3 eggs, separated
3 tablespoons raspberry jam

Preparation time: 35 minutes plus standing and cooling
Cooking time: about 1 hour 10 minutes
Oven: 160°C, 325°F, Gas Mark 3; then 120°C, 250°F, Gas Mark ½

1. Heat the milk with the lemon peel in a small pan. When it reaches boiling point, remove from the heat and stand, covered, for 10 minutes. Then discard the lemon peel and replace the pan of milk over gentle heat. Add the butter and 25 g (1 oz) of the sugar, stirring till they have melted, then remove from the heat and stir in the breadcrumbs.
2. Cool for 10 minutes, then stir in the lightly beaten egg yolks. Pour into a buttered baking dish and bake in a preheated moderate oven for 30 minutes.
3. Take the pudding out of the oven and turn the oven down to very cool.
4. Warm the jam and spread it over the surface of the pudding. Beat the egg whites until firm, and fold in the remaining caster sugar to make a meringue mixture. Spread this over the jam so that

the pudding is entirely covered.
5. Return the pudding to the oven for another 30 minutes, or until the meringue is firm and lightly coloured. Serve hot, warm, or at room temperature, with cream.

LEFT, Queen of puddings; RIGHT, Fresh fruit salad

WINE JELLY

MAKES 1 × 600 ml (1 pint) JELLY
100 g (4 oz) sugar
225 g (8 oz) redcurrant jelly
grated rind and juice of 1 orange
grated rind and juice of 1 lemon
½ bottle red wine
1½ packets (20 g /¾ oz) gelatine

Preparation time: about 15 minutes plus setting overnight
Cooking time: about 10 minutes

1. Put the sugar in a small pan with 150 ml (¼ pint) water. Add the redcurrant jelly, the grated rind and the juice of the orange and the lemon. Heat gently, and stir until the sugar has melted.
2. Pour through a strainer to get rid of any lumps, and return to the clean pan. Pour in the red wine and stir over gentle heat till all is mixed. Melt the gelatine in 65 ml (2½ fl oz) hot water and add to the mixture. Stir over a low heat till blended smoothly, and strain once more.
3. Pour into a 600 ml (1 pint) jelly mould and leave to cool. Set in the refrigerator overnight, and turn out on to a flat platter to serve, with a bowl of lightly whipped double or whipping cream if you like.

Variation: for a pretty centrepiece, set the jelly in a ring mould, turn out on to a flat platter and fill the centre with lightly whipped cream.

SEVEN CUP PUDDING

SERVES 6–8
1 teacup soft white breadcrumbs
1 teacup shredded suet
1 teacup sultanas
1 teacup currants
1 teacup sugar
1 teacup flour
50 g (2 oz) chopped mixed peel
50 g (2 oz) coarsely chopped or grated almonds
2 teaspoons ground ginger
1 teaspoon ground cinnamon
1 teaspoon mixed spice
a pinch of salt
1 egg
approx 150 ml (¼ pint) milk
1 teaspoon baking soda
1 teaspoon wine vinegar

Preparation time: about 30 minutes
Cooking time: 4–6 hours

This is an old-fashioned pudding recipe which my Scottish grandmother gave to my mother when she married. It is an excellent spicy pudding, less rich and heavy than a plum pudding, but can be used as a substitute for one if required, with brandy butter instead of custard sauce. The measurements are based on volume rather than weight; choose a teacup holding about 175 ml (6 fluid ounces) as your measure.

1. Grease well a 900 ml (1½ pint) pudding basin.
2. Mix all the ingredients together except for the egg, milk, baking soda and vinegar.
3. Break the egg into a measuring jug and make up to 175 ml (6 fl oz) with milk. Stir into the mixture.
4. Dissolve the baking soda in the vinegar for a few moments, then stir into the pudding mixture.
5. Mix all together well, then pour into the prepared pudding basin and steam covered, set in a large pan of boiling water half-way up the sides of the bowl, for 4–6 hours.
6. Turn out and serve with Custard sauce (page 70) or Brandy butter (page 9).

TOP, Wine jelly; BOTTOM, Seven cup pudding

PRUNE JELLY

MAKES 1 × 600 ml (1 pint) JELLY
1 tablespoon caster sugar
475 ml (16 fl oz) prune juice
2 tablespoons lemon juice
2 tablespoons orange juice
1 × 15 g (½ oz) packet gelatine
300 ml (½ pint) double cream, lightly
   whipped

Preparation time: about 15 minutes

1. Add the sugar to the prune juice, then the fruit juices. Melt the gelatine in 65 ml (2½ fl oz) hot water and mix with the juices.
2. Pour through a strainer into a 600 ml (1 pint) ring mould and chill in the refrigerator. As it is already cold it will only take a couple of hours to set.
3. Turn out on to a flat plate and fill the centre with the cream.

RASPBERRY MERINGUE

MAKES 1 × 18 cm (7 inch) MERINGUE
3 egg whites
175 g (6 oz) caster sugar
2 packets frozen raspberries without sugar
300 ml (½ pint) double cream, lightly
   whipped

Preparation time: about 20 minutes, plus cooling
Cooking time: 2 hours
Oven: 110°C, 225°F, Gas Mark ¼

1. Line a baking sheet with non-stick silicone paper.
2. Beat the egg whites until stiff, then fold in the sifted caster sugar gradually, continuing to beat until the mixture is thick and creamy.
3. Spoon the mixture on to the prepared baking sheet. Smooth out slightly with a palette knife into a thick circle about 18 cm (7 inches) across.
4. Put the meringue in the middle of a preheated oven and leave for 2 hours, watching occasionally to make sure all is well. If it colours unevenly, it should be turned round from time to time. It should turn a delicate straw colour, nothing darker. Remove from the oven and cool.
5. Remove the meringue from the silicone paper very carefully, as it is quite delicate, lay it on a flat dish and cover with the lightly whipped cream which will camouflage any cracks.
6. Take the raspberries out of the freezer 1 hour beforehand so they are only just defrosted and lay them one by one on top of the cream. If the meringue breaks into several pieces, break it up even more, and make layers of meringue pieces, whipped cream, and raspberries in a soufflé dish. This makes just as good a pudding and is only slightly less pretty.

TOP, Prune jelly; BOTTOM, Raspberry meringue

PARTY FARE

Entertaining family and friends is perhaps the most joyful part of Christmas, and food in party guise is the theme of this chapter. Here are recipes designed to serve large numbers of people, to provide memorable meals for more intimate numbers, or to make eye-catching centre-pieces on the party buffet table.

A MIXED SALAD

SERVES 4–6

a few inner leaves of red oak leaf lettuce, or Cos, or Webbs, torn in pieces

a few inner leaves of curly endive, or batavia, torn in pieces

a few inner leaves of radicchio, torn in pieces

inner part of 1 medium fennel, halved and thinly sliced

½ cucumber, peeled and cut in 4 lengthways, then sliced

1 yellow pepper, cut in strips

Dressing:
sea salt
freshly ground black pepper
a pinch of sugar
¾ tablespoon lemon juice
¾ tablespoon white wine vinegar
2 tablespoons olive oil
1 tablespoon hazelnut oil

Preparation time: 20 minutes plus chilling

This pretty salad makes an excellent dish to serve alone, or as the accompaniment to meat dishes. Try to achieve a nicely balanced mixture of red and green leaves for the main body of the salad, and discard all tough outer leaves.

1. Assemble the tender red and green leaves in a salad bowl and mix gently. Scatter the thinly sliced fennel over them. Spread the little pieces of cucumber over the fennel, and finally, the strips of yellow pepper over all.

2. Cover with a cloth and chill in the refrigerator till ready to serve, or for at least 1 hour.

3. Put the salt, pepper and sugar in a small bowl, and add the lemon juice and white wine vinegar. Beat until they are blended, then stir in the two oils. (If you have a flavoured vinegar, you can use this instead of the white wine vinegar. At present, I am using a blackcurrant vinegar, or an elderflower vinegar.)

4. Just before serving, beat the dressing once more and pour over the salad. Toss it at the table.

FISH CHOWDER

25 g (1 oz) butter, melted
1 onion, peeled and finely chopped
750 g (1½ lb) fresh haddock fillets, skinned
450 g (1 lb) potatoes, peeled and sliced (approx 5mm/¼ inch thick)
sea salt
freshly ground black pepper
300 ml (½ pint) single cream
50 g (2 oz) streaky bacon rashers (or 3 tablespoons chopped parsley)

Preparation time: 30 minutes
Cooking time: about 45 minutes

A meal in itself, this dish should be served in soup plates, and only needs a salad to follow it.

1. Put the melted butter in the bottom of a heavy flameproof casserole. Add the onion.

2. Cut the fish fillets in neat pieces and lay them on top of the onion.

3. Lay the potato slices over the fish, seasoning each layer with salt and pepper.

4. Add enough cold water to just cover the surface of the potatoes and bring to the boil. Cover the pan and simmer gently for 40 minutes. When the potatoes are cooked, heat the cream and pour it in. Stir very gently to mix without breaking up the pieces of fish and the potato slices, and season with more salt and pepper as needed.

5. Chop the bacon rashers and fry gently until crisp. Scatter them over the top of the dish and serve it with water biscuits – matzos are best. Alternatively, the fried bacon can be replaced by 3 tablespoons of finely chopped parsley.

TOP, A Mixed salad; BOTTOM, Fish chowder

PROVENÇAL SOUP WITH PISTOU

SERVES 8–10

1 medium onion, peeled and chopped
2 small leeks, chopped
2 small carrots, chopped
175 g (6 oz) courgettes
175 g (6 oz) string beans
6 tablespoons olive oil
1.2 litres (2 pints) hot water
100 g (4 oz) haricot beans, soaked and pre-
  cooked for 20 minutes
sea salt
freshly ground black pepper
225 g (8 oz) tomatoes, skinned and chopped
50 g (2 oz) short macaroni

Pistou:

3 cloves garlic, peeled
40 g (1½ oz) finely chopped fresh basil leaves
50 g (2 oz) Parmesan cheese, freshly grated
4 tablespoons olive oil

Preparation time: 25 minutes plus
standing
Cooking time: 1 hour 20 minutes

The 'pistou' in this recipe is a sauce widely used in southern France, which is a variation of the famous 'pesto', or basil sauce of Genoa in Italy.

1. Keep the prepared onion, leeks and carrots separate. Cut the unpeeled courgettes in slices 1 cm (½ in) thick. Cut the string beans in 2.5 cm (1 in) pieces.
2. Heat the oil in a heavy pan and cook the onion and leeks until softened and pale golden. Add the hot water, carrots and haricot beans. (Canned haricot beans may be used as an alternative, in which case add them when the other vegetables are cooked.) Bring to the boil, add salt and pepper, and simmer for 45 minutes. Add the courgettes, string beans and tomatoes and simmer for a further 20 minutes. Add the macaroni and cook for about 15 minutes longer, until tender.
3. While the soup is cooking, make the pistou. Chop the garlic very finely and pound it to a pulp in a mortar. Add the basil leaves to the garlic. Pound again until the garlic and basil are amalgamated. Add

the grated cheese and continue pounding. When all is smooth, beat in the oil, drop by drop.
4. When all has blended into a smooth paste, put the pistou in a warm tureen and pour the boiling soup over it. Cover and stand for 5 minutes.

POTATO SALAD

675 g (1½ lb) new or waxy potatoes
3 tablespoons olive oil
1 tablespoon white wine vinegar
freshly ground black pepper
sea salt
2 tablespoons chopped fresh parsley
2 tablespoons chopped fresh chives

Preparation time: about 15 minutes plus
cooling
Cooking time: 20 minutes

1. Wash the potatoes and cook them in their skins in boiling salted water. Drain and skin them as soon as they are cool enough to handle. Cut them into thick slices or quarters, according to size.
2. Pour over the oil and vinegar while the potatoes are still hot, as this helps the

flavours blend well, and add black pepper and more salt as needed. Stir in the chopped herbs and serve soon after cooling; do not chill.

LEFT, Provençal soup with pistou; RIGHT, Potato salad

FENNEL GRATIN

4 heads fennel
450 ml (¾ pint) milk
1 slice onion (not too thick)
2 cloves
½ bay leaf
sea salt
6 black peppercorns
a pinch of nutmeg or mace
25 g (1 oz) butter
1 tablespoon plain flour
150 ml (¼ pint) single cream
100 g (4 oz) Gruyère cheese, grated

Preparation time: 10 minutes, plus standing
Cooking time: 40 minutes
Oven (optional): 200°F, 400°C, Gas Mark 6

This dish of fennel in a creamy sauce makes a good first course, or even a main dish for a fairly light, or vegetarian meal.
1. Trim the fennel, drop into a large pan of lightly salted boiling water and simmer for 30 minutes, or until tender.
2. For the sauce, put the milk in a small pan with the onion, cloves, bay leaf, salt and peppercorns, nutmeg or mace. Bring to the boil slowly, remove from the heat and stand, covered, for 20 minutes.
3. When the time is up, melt the butter in a clean pan and add the flour. Cook gently for 1–2 minutes, stirring. Strain the flavoured milk and gradually add it to the roux, stirring till blended. Simmer gently for 3 minutes, stirring often to prevent it turning lumpy. Add the cream and most of the grated cheese, stirring till smooth, and add salt and pepper as needed.

4. When the fennel are tender, drain them well and cut each head in half. Lay them in a shallow gratin dish and pour the sauce over them. Scatter the remaining cheese over the top, and brown briefly under the grill. (Alternatively, the dish can be made in advance, and reheated for 25 minutes in a moderately hot oven.)

HERB PÂTÉ

450 g (1 lb) belly of pork
225 g (8 oz) unsmoked bacon
100 g (4 oz) pig's liver
1 medium onion, peeled and chopped
2 cloves garlic, peeled and crushed
sea salt
freshly ground black pepper
6 juniper berries, crushed
225 g (8 oz) spinach
100 g (4 oz) sorrel
50 g (2 oz) chopped fresh parsley
50 g (2 oz) chopped mixed fresh herbs:
    chervil, dill, tarragon, lovage, marjoram,
    lemon, thyme and sage
1 large egg
juice of ½ lemon

Preparation time: about 25 minutes plus cooling and weighting
Cooking time: about 1 hour 20 minutes
Oven: 180°C, 350°F, Gas Mark 4

For this recipe, ask your butcher to mince the pork, bacon and liver for you.
1. Put all the meats together in a large bowl and add the onion and garlic. Add salt and pepper to taste, and the juniper berries.
2. Blanch the spinach and sorrel for 4 minutes in boiling salted water; drain in a colander, pressing out as much moisture as possible, then chop fairly finely and stir into the meat mixture. Stir the chopped parsley and the chopped mixed herbs into the mixture. Beat the egg lightly and stir it in, adding the lemon juice.
3. Turn into an ovenproof dish or tin mould and cover with foil. Put in a roasting pan half full of hot water and cook for approximately 1 hour 20 minutes in a preheated oven. When done the pâté will have shrunk away from the edges of the container.

4. Cool for 1 hour, then lay a 1 kg (2 lb) weight on top and leave until completely cold. Store in the refrigerator. Turn out on a flat dish to serve, with toast or French bread and butter.

LEFT, Fennel gratin; RIGHT, Herb pâté

EGGS IN TARRAGON JELLY

4 eggs
4 sprigs tarragon
450 ml (¾ pint) chicken stock
2½ teaspoons gelatine
4 lettuce leaves

Preparation time: 15 minutes, plus infusing, cooling and setting
Cooking time: about 25 minutes

1. Bring a saucepan of lightly salted water to the boil. Put the eggs into the pan and cook them for exactly 5 minutes. Cool the eggs immediately under cold water, and shell them carefully.
2. Strip four of the best leaves from the tarragon sprigs and reserve them. Heat the stock (which must be of a good flavour and totally free from fat) with the tarragon sprigs. When it boils, draw the pan to the side of the stove and cover it. Leave for 15 minutes to infuse. If the flavour still seems weak, bring back to the boil and leave to cool once more.
3. Lift out the tarragon and stir in the gelatine. Stir the stock over a very low heat until the gelatine has melted. Pour through a strainer to make a thin layer in each of 4 ramekin or similar dishes.

4. Put in the refrigerator to set. When firm, lay a tarragon leaf on the bottom of each one, then an egg, then one or two more tarragon leaves, if you like. Pour the remaining stock through a strainer to cover the eggs. Chill until set.
5. To serve, turn out on to individual plates and surround with shredded lettuce.

RABBIT PÂTÉ

SERVES 6–8
225 g (8 oz) boneless rabbit
225 g (8 oz) belly of pork
100 g (1 oz) pie veal
100 g (4 oz) fat unsmoked bacon
1 clove garlic, peeled
2 teaspoons sea salt
1 teaspoon black peppercorns
12 juniper berries
¼ teaspoon mace
1½ tablespoons chopped parsley
1 teaspoon chopped fresh sage
1 teaspoon chopped fresh thyme
1 egg, lightly beaten
2 tablespoons brandy
150 ml (¼ pint) white wine

Preparation time: about 25 minutes plus cooling, weighting and chilling
Cooking time: 1 hour 20 minutes – 1¾ hours
Oven: 160°C, 325°F, Gas Mark 3

One small pâté can be stored for future use by sealing with a layer of melted lard (pork fat) after cooling; you will need enough lard to cover the top of the pâté completely with a layer of lard about 6 mm (¼ inch) thick. Once sealed, the pâté can be kept in a cool place for up to 8 weeks. Turn out to serve, cutting away the fat surround.
1. Put the rabbit through the mincer with the pork, veal and bacon. Mix them all together in a big bowl. Crush the garlic in a mortar with the salt, peppercorns, juniper berries and mace. Add to the meat. Stir in the chopped herbs and the egg, then the brandy and the wine.
2. Pile into an ovenproof dish or tin mould and stand in a roasting pan half full of hot water. Bake for 1¾ hours in a preheated moderate oven. Alternatively cook in 2 small dishes, allowing 1 hour 20 minutes.
3. Remove from the oven and when half cooled, weigh down with a 1 kg (2 lb) weight (for the large pâté). Chill in the refrigerator for 2 to 3 days before serving.

Variation: for a venison pâté, follow the recipe for rabbit pâté, substituting venison for rabbit.

TOP, Eggs in tarragon jelly; BOTTOM, Rabbit pâté

WINTER SALAD

250 g (9 oz) Chinese cabbage, or white
    cabbage
100 g (4 oz) carrots, scraped
2 stalks celery, washed and trimmed
1 crisp eating apple, cored but not peeled
1½ tablespoons lemon juice
3 tablespoons sunflower seed oil
50 g (2 oz) almonds, hazelnuts, or pecans

Preparation time: 10–15 minutes

Served on its own this salad makes a good first course, with hard-boiled eggs to accompany it, it becomes a light but satisfying main dish.
1. Slice the cabbage reasonably finely. Grate the carrots and chop the celery and apple. Mix all together in a bowl.
2. Stir in the lemon juice and sunflower seed oil.
3. Chop the nuts and scatter them over the salad. Salt and pepper will not be necessary.

THREE-BEAN SALAD

SERVES 4–6
100 g (4 oz) French or Italian dried haricot
    beans
100 g (4 oz) green dried flageolets
100 g (4 oz) dried red kidney beans
salt
freshly ground black pepper
olive oil
white wine vinegar
1 Spanish onion, peeled
4 tablespoons chopped fresh parsley

Preparation time: 15 minutes, plus
soaking
Cooking time: about 30–40 minutes

This salad is best eaten within an hour or so of cooking, before it has completely cooled.
1. Each of the three types of beans must be cooked separately. Either soak them in separate bowls for 2–3 hours, or bring them to the boil in a pan covered with cold water, turn off the heat and leave covered for 1 hour.
2. Drain away the water, cover the beans with fresh cold water and cook (still in separate saucepans) until tender, boiling briskly for 10 minutes before simmering. Add salt only towards the end of the cooking.
3. When the beans are tender, drain them in a colander and rinse briefly.
4. Mix all the beans together in a bowl and add salt and pepper to taste. Add enough olive oil to moisten the salad well without leaving a pool in the bottom of the bowl, and about one-third as much white wine vinegar.
5. Cut the Spanish onion in quarters, then cut each piece in thin slices, and divide each slice into thin strips. Stir into the beans and mix well. Add the chopped parsley, stirring in some of it, and leaving some to be sprinkled on top of the salad as a garnish.

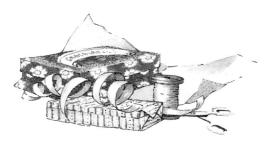

LEFT, Winter salad; RIGHT, Three-bean salad

COLD POACHED BASS WITH HERBS

1 sea bass, about 1 kg (2 lb)
1 onion, peeled and halved
1 carrot halved
1 stick celery, halved
1 bay leaf
3 stalks parsley
3 sprigs lovage
2 tablespoons white wine vinegar
1 tablespoon sea salt
10 black peppercorns
225 g (8 oz) tomatoes
1 bunch spring onions
1 tablespoon olive oil
3 tablespoons lemon juice
3 tablespoons chopped mixed fresh herbs:
   chervil, dill, tarragon, parsley and chives

Preparation time: 30 minutes plus
cooling
Cooking time: 50 minutes

1. Put the fish in a pan that fits it as neatly as possible (a fish kettle would be ideal) and cover with cold water. Lift out the bass. Put the onion, carrot and celery in the pan with the bay leaf, parsley stalks, lovage, vinegar, salt and peppercorns. Bring slowly to the boil and simmer gently for 30 minutes. Leave to cool.
2. Return the bass to the pan and bring back to the boil. Simmer for 20 minutes. Remove the pan from the heat and leave the fish to cool in the liquid. An hour or two later, lift out the fish and carefully remove the skin. Lay the bass on a serving platter.

3. Skin the tomatoes and chop them, discarding any juice. Slice the spring onions and mix them with the chopped tomatoes in a bowl. Add a little salt and pepper, the olive oil and 1 tablespoon of the lemon juice. Mix lightly then lay all around the fish. Pour the remaining lemon juice over the fish, and scatter the dish with the chopped herbs.
4. Serve with hollandaise sauce with herbs (see below), or simply with lemons cut into quarters. For a spectacular-looking dish, garnish with a selection of shellfish.

HOLLANDAISE SAUCE WITH HERBS

3 egg yolks
pinch of sea salt
100 g (4 oz) butter
1 tablespoon lemon juice
3 tablespoons chopped mixed fresh herbs:
   chervil, dill, tarragon and chives

Preparation time: about 15 minutes

This sauce is excellent for many kinds of poached fish, shellfish, poached eggs, asparagus, broccoli or artichokes.
1. This tricky sauce is quickly made in a food processor or blender. Have the container heated by filling with hot water and standing for a few minutes; drain and dry.
2. Break the egg yolks with the salt into the food processor bowl. Heat the butter until almost boiling, then add the lemon juice. Turn on the food processor, and pour in the butter slowly through the lid. Stop as soon as it is amalgamated. Spoon into a bowl, stir in the chopped herbs and serve immediately.

3. The sauce can be kept warm for a short time, if absolutely necessary, by standing the bowl over hot water, but do not attempt to reheat it.

Cold poached bass with Hollandaise sauce

CURRIED CHICKEN WITH CORIANDER

1 onion, peeled and halved
1 carrot, coarsely chopped
1 stick celery, coarsely chopped
1.5 kg (3½ lb) roasting chicken
1 bay leaf
3 sprigs parsley
3 sprigs lovage
1 teaspoon sea salt
6 black peppercorns

Curry sauce:
3 tablespoons desiccated coconut
50 g (2 oz) butter
1 large onion, peeled and finely chopped
2 cloves garlic, peeled and crushed
1 tablespoon mild curry powder
¼ teaspoon ground turmeric
¼ teaspoon ground cumin seed
¼ teaspoon ground coriander
pinch of ground chilli
1 tablespoon redcurrant jelly
juice of 1 lime or ½ lemon
1 tablespoon plain flour
4 tablespoons plain unsweetened yogurt
2 tablespoons chopped almonds
2 tablespoons chopped fresh coriander or 3
   tablespoons chopped fresh basil

Preparation time: 40 minutes plus
cooling
Cooking time: about 1 hour 30 minutes

1. Put the vegetables in a saucepan with the chicken, bay leaf, parsley, lovage, salt and peppercorns. Pour in enough cold water just to cover the chicken, bring to the boil and poach for 1 hour. Lift out the chicken when it is tender. When the chicken is cool enough to handle, remove all the skin and bones and discard them. Cut the meat into neat small pieces. Set aside.
2. Strain the liquid in which the chicken was cooked, discarding the vegetables and herbs. Taste the stock: if it is too weak, reduce it by fast boiling until it has a good flavour. Measure out 600 ml (1 pint). If any stock remains, reserve it for another dish or for soup.
3. To make the curry sauce, pour half of the measured stock over the desiccated coconut in a bowl and leave for 15 minutes

to form a coconut 'milk'. Melt the butter in a large saucepan and cook the chopped onion gently until pale golden, adding the garlic halfway through. Sprinkle on the curry powder and spices, stirring all the time, and cook for a minute or two. Pour on the remaining 300 ml (½ pint) stock and stir until blended.
4. Simmer gently for 15 minutes, then add the redcurrant jelly through a sieve and the lime or lemon juice. Pour the coconut 'milk' through a sieve into the curry sauce, pushing lightly with the back of a wooden spoon to extract all the liquid. Stir the flour into the yogurt to make a smooth paste and add it to the curry sauce by degrees, continuing to stir until all is blended.
5. Add the chicken pieces to the sauce. Reheat, stirring, and finally add the chopped nuts and the coriander (or basil). Stand, covered, for 5 minutes before serving. Accompany with plain boiled rice.

COLD CHICKEN WITH HERB DRESSING

1.5 kg (3½ lb) roasting chicken
1 onion, peeled and halved
1 carrot, scrubbed
1 leek, sliced lengthways
1 bay leaf
3 sprigs parsley
3 sprigs lovage
2 sprigs thyme
sea salt

Herb dressing:
1 egg yolk
1 tablespoon Dijon mustard
150 ml (¼ pint) olive oil
pinch of sea salt
1 teaspoon white wine vinegar
1 teaspoon lemon juice
4 tablespoons plain unsweetened yogurt
2 tablespoons chopped dill
2 tablespoons chopped chervil

Preparation time: about 45 minutes plus chilling overnight and for 1 hour before serving
Cooking time: about 2 hours

1. Start to prepare this dish the day before you plan to serve it. Put the chicken in a saucepan that will just hold it nicely and cover with cold water. Remove the bird. Add the vegetables to the cold water with the herbs and some salt. Bring almost to the boil and cover the pan. Cook for 30 minutes, then put the chicken back into the saucepan, bring back to the boil, cover and simmer gently for 1 hour. Lift out the chicken and leave to cool.

2. Continue to boil the remaining contents of the pan until you have reduced it to a small amount of strongly flavoured stock, tasting frequently to see that it does not get too salty. Strain the stock and leave it to cool, then chill it in the refrigerator overnight.

3. Make the dressing the next day. Remove all fat from the surface of the stock. Make a mayonnaise: put the egg yolk, which must be at room temperature, into a bowl with the mustard and whisk in the oil drop by drop until thick. Whisk in the lemon juice, then remaining oil followed by the salt and vinegar. Mix together with the yogurt. Stir in 4 tablespoons of the chicken stock which will have set to a jelly. Beat until smooth, or purée briefly in a blender, then stir in the chopped herbs.

4. Carve the chicken into joints or slices free from bone, as you prefer. Lay them on a flat dish and spoon the dressing over them. Put the dish in the refrigerator and chill the chicken for 1 hour before serving. Excellent accompaniments for this dish would be a potato salad in a vinaigrette dressing and a green salad.

POULTRY AT CHRISTMAS
Before turkey came to be the bird favoured to dominate the Christmas dinner table early in the 16th century, soon after it was brought to Europe from the New World, many other birds had been given this honour over the centuries. Goose, chicken (cockerel) and pheasant were among birds to be found on the dinner tables of ordinary folk, while peacocks and swans were reserved for the tables of the rich. The roasted peacock was often brought in procession into the Great Hall, its feathers rearranged over its body, its beak painted gold and propped open with a brandy-soaked piece of bread which would be set alight just before the bird was carried in.

BRAISED BEEF WITH GLAZED VEGETABLES

SERVES 6

1.5 kg (3 lb) topside of beef
1 large onion, peeled and sliced
2 large carrots, sliced
2 garlic cloves, peeled
2 bay leaves
2 sprigs thyme
1 bottle red wine
40 g (1½ oz) butter
1 tablespoon olive oil
100 g (4 oz) mushrooms, coarsely chopped
1 calf's foot, split in 4
sea salt
freshly ground black pepper

To garnish:
12 small onions, peeled
225 g (8 oz) thin carrots, cut in 3
25 g (1 oz) butter
1 tablespoon sugar

Preparation time: 40 minutes, plus
marinating overnight
Cooking time: about 3 hours
Oven: 160°C, 325°F, Gas Mark 3

A joint of good beef, braise in red wine, and garnished with glazed carrots and onions makes a very festive dish ad requires little in the way of accompaniment: just a potato purée, or some fresh noodles, with a green salad.

1. Start 1 day in advance. Put the beef in a deep dish with the sliced vegetables scattered over it, adding the whole garlic cloves and herbs. Pour over the wine and leave overnight in a cool place, basting once or twice.

2. Next day, remove the beef from the marinade and wipe it with kitchen paper. Strain the wine, reserving it and the sliced vegetables and herbs.

3. Melt the butter and oil in a fireproof casserole and brown the meat all over. Then remove it, and put the sliced vegetables in the pan. Add the chopped mushrooms and cook gently for 4 minutes, stirring all the time, then replace the beef, with the calf's foot pieces tucked around it Heat the marinade and pour it over, adding salt and pepper. Bring to the boil, cover, transfer to a preheated oven and cook for 2½ hours

4. About 30 minutes before the time is up, put the onions and carrots for the garnish in a small pan. Take about 300 ml (½ pint) stock from the casserole with a bulb-type baster, and pour over the vegetables. There should be enough to come level with the vegetables. Bring to the boil and cook quite fast, covered, until the vegetables are tender, about 15–20 minutes, then drain them, reserving any stock that remains.

5. Put the butter and sugar into the vegetable pan, adding 2 tablespoons of the vegetable stock and cook all together gently, shaking from time to time, until the sauce has become reduced to a sticky glaze and the vegetables have slightly browned.

6. When the meat has finished cooking, remove it and carve it in fairly thick slices. Strain the stock, and lay the sliced vegetables in a shallow dish. Discard the calf's foot, garlic, and herbs. Lay the sliced beef over the vegetables, with the glazed carrots and onions along the sides of the dish. Moisten the meat with a little of the stock from the vegetables. Remove the fat from the main body of stock and reduce it a little by fast boiling. Serve separately, in a sauceboat.

CANNELLONI WITH TWO SAUCES

SERVES 8

Pasta:
2 whole eggs plus 2 egg whites
2 tablespoons olive oil
½ tablespoon water
a pinch of salt
350 g (12 oz) plain flour

Filling:
450 g (1 lb) spinach, washed and drained
750 g (1½ lb) ricotta
2 egg yolks
75–100 g (3–4 oz) grated Parmesan
sea salt
freshly ground black pepper

Tomato sauce:
1 small onion, peeled and chopped
25 g (1 oz) butter
1 tablespoon olive oil
1 clove garlic, peeled and chopped
750 g (1½ lb) tomatoes, skinned and chopped
salt
freshly ground black pepper
2 tablespoons fresh basil, cut in strips, or ½
    teaspoon dried oregano

Béchamel sauce:
50 g (2 oz) butter
4 tablespoons plain flour
300 ml (½ pint) chicken (or vegetable) stock
300 ml (½ pint) single cream
sea salt
freshly ground black pepper

To garnish:
25 g (1 oz) freshly grated Parmesan

Preparation time: about 1 hour 30
minutes, plus cooling
Cooking time: 50–60 minutes
Oven: 190°C, 375°F, Gas Mark 5

A big dish of cannelloni makes a festive Boxing Day lunch, and needs only a green salad as accompaniment. This version could well figure in a vegetarian meal, since it is not based on meat. The pasta may be made at home, or, if you are not an accomplished pasta maker, armed with a food processor and pasta mill, you could simply buy freshly made sheets of pasta. Allow 100–175 g (4–6 oz) per person.

1. For the pasta, put the eggs, 1 tablespoon of the oil, water and salt in a food processor and process for 30 seconds. (Unless you have a large machine, this is best done in two batches.) Add the flour and process for another 30 seconds. Turn out on to a floured piece of cling film, wrap up, and rest for 5 minutes. If you do not have a processor, you could, of course, mix the pasta ingredients by hand in a bowl.

2. Feed the pasta dough through the pasta mill three times through the widest roller, folding in three each time. Then feed it through progressively narrower rollers, once through each, until you reach the narrowest gauge but one. This will be thin enough.

3. Cut the dough into strips about 6 × 7.5 cm (2½ × 3 inches). Drop them, 5 or 6 at a time, into a broad pan of boiling water; cook for 4–5 minutes, then lift out and drop into a bowl of cold water with the remaining oil in it. Leave for a few moments, then lift out and lay on a cloth to drain.

4. To make the filling, drop the spinach into lightly boiling salted water, cook for 5 minutes and drain in a colander. When it is cool enough to handle, squeeze out any excess moisture, lay it on a board, and chop it roughly by hand.

5. Put the spinach in a food processor or blender with the ricotta, egg yolks, Parmesan, salt and pepper and process till well blended. (Alternatively, chop the

spinach finely, rather than roughly, before mixing it with the ricotta, egg yolks, Parmesan, salt and pepper.) Chill the mixture.

6. To make the tomato sauce, cook the onion in the butter and oil, adding the garlic after 4–5 minutes. When they start to soften, add the tomatoes. Season the sauce with salt and pepper and cook gently for about 20 minutes, until it is a good thick consistency. Stir in the basil, or oregano, and set aside.

7. To make the Béchamel sauce, melt the butter in a small pan, add the flour and cook for 1 minute, stirring. Heat the stock and cream together and pour on to the roux, stirring until smooth. Simmer for 3 minutes, stirring often, adding salt and pepper to taste.

8. To assemble the cannelloni, put a thin roll of the filling on each strip of pasta, roll up, and lay in a lightly buttered rectangular baking dish. Ideally, the dish should be large enough to hold all the rolls in one layer. Then pour the tomato sauce over them. (If you have to assemble them in two layers, put some of the tomato sauce between each layer, as well as on top.) Then pour the Béchamel sauce over all, sprinkle with Parmesan, and bake for 30 minutes in a preheated oven. If prepared in advance, allow 40 minutes at the same temperature.

REDCURRANT SNOW

150 ml (¼ pint) double cream
2 egg whites
150 ml (¼ pint) plain, unsweetened yogurt
2 tablespoons caster sugar
450 g (1 lb) redcurrants
2 tablespoons chopped fresh mint

Preparation time: 25 minutes

1. Whip the cream until thick but not dry. Beat the egg whites until stiff. Beat the yogurt until smooth. Mix the egg whites and then the yogurt into the cream, folding them in lightly. Stir in the sugar.
2. Wash and drain the redcurrants. Pull the berries off the stalks and fold into the cream. Stir in the chopped mint and serve soon after making.

Variation: for blueberry snow, the same quantity of blueberries may be used instead of the redcurrants.

RASPBERRY TRIFLE

SERVES 5–6
1 sponge cake, slightly stale, or 8 trifle
  sponges
juice of 1 large orange (or 5 tablespoons
  medium dry sherry, Madeira or Marsala)
3 egg yolks
4 tablespoons caster sugar
300 ml (½ pint) milk
225 g (8 oz) raspberries fresh or frozen, or
  225 g (8 oz) raspberry jam
300 ml (½ pint) whipping cream

To serve:
chopped pistaccio nuts
crystallised rose petals

Preparation time: about 20 minutes plus soaking, cooling and chilling
Cooking time: about 10 minutes

When made with whole berries this makes a very delicious party pudding.
1. Cut the sponge cake, or trifle sponges into thick chunks and use to line a broad shallow bowl, preferably glass. Pour the orange juice or alcohol, if using, over them and leave for a little so the sponge can absorb it.
2. Beat the egg yolks in a china bowl, using an electric hand beater, rotary beater, or wire whisk. Shake in the caster sugar while beating, and continue until you have a smooth creamy paste.
3. Choose a pan into which the bowl fits nicely, half fill it with water, and bring it to simmering point on the stove.
4. Heat the milk in a small pan until boiling, then pour it on to the egg yolks, beating constantly. Stand the bowl in the saucepan over simmering water and continue to beat until it has slightly thickened, so that it coats the back of the wooden spoon lightly. Stand the bowl in a sink half full of cold water to cool quickly, stirring every now and then to prevent a skin forming.
5. If using raspberry jam, spread it over the sponge cakes now, then pour the cool custard over them. If using fresh (or frozen) raspberries, pour the custard over first, then scatter the berries over it. If possible, stand the bowl in the refrigerator for an hour or two at this stage.
6. Then whip the cream and spread it over the berries. If possible, chill again for an hour or two before serving. Just before serving, scatter chopped pistaccio nuts and crystallised rose petals over the top. To crystallise the petals, dip them first in lightly beaten egg white, then in caster sugar. Shake off any excess sugar and leave to dry before using them on the trifle. Rose petals are, of course, edible and also look very pretty on the trifle. You could put chocolate curls on the trifle, if you prefer.

LEFT, Red currant snow; RIGHT, Raspberry trifle

CHRISTMAS DRINKS

The cheerful tradition of the steaming wassail
bowl, redolent of spices and alcohol, is upheld in
this chapter, though not all the drinks are
alcoholic, and there is a mixture
of deliciously cooling as
well as splendidly
warming ones.

CIDER CUP

SERVES 6–8

65 ml (2½ fl oz) sugar syrup (see below)
65 ml (2½ oz) lemon juice
150 ml (¼ pint) orange juice
50 ml (2 fl oz) applejack or calvados (for a
    slightly stronger cup)
8 ice cubes
1 litre (1¾ pint) dry cider
½ orange, sliced
½ lemon, sliced
4 strips cucumber peel, or borage in season
a few maraschino cherries, or strawberries in
    season

Preparation time: 15 minutes, plus
chilling

1. Mix the sugar syrup, fruit juices, and applejack or calvados (if using) in a large jug and chill for two hours in the refrigerator. Have the cider also chilling.
2. When ready to serve, put about 8 ice cubes in the jug and pour over the cider. Add the fruit and cucumber or borage, stir well and serve.

MULLED WINE

SERVES 6–8

the peel of 1 lemon
the peel of 1 orange
6 cloves
1 stick cinnamon
½ whole nutmeg
12 lumps sugar
300 ml (½) cold water
1½ bottles red wine
1 liqueur glass brandy (optional)

Preparation time: about 10 minutes
Cooking time: 10–15 minutes

This hot mulled wine is as near as most of us get to drinking the traditional 'wassail' at Christmas. Wassail was a toast, at least as old as Saxon times, and for centuries it was customary to have the wassail bowl steaming on table or sideboard throughout Christmas. Its traditional content was ale and the pulp of roasted apples, plus sugar and spices.
1. Put the lemon and orange peel, the cloves, cinnamon, nutmeg and sugar in a saucepan with the water. Bring to the boil and cook till the sugar has dissolved.
2. Add the wine and bring back to just below boiling point. Add the brandy at this point, if you are using it. Strain into a hot jug or bowl and serve in warmed glasses.

SUGAR SYRUP

Sugar Syrup is used in several of the drinks in this chapter; it is much better to use in cold drinks than dry sugar, which does not dissolve satisfactorily and thus fails to sweeten the drink.

To make sugar syrup, put 100 g (4 oz) sugar and 150 ml (¼ pint) cold water in a small saucepan and bring to the boil. Simmer for 2–3 minutes, until the sugar has completely dissolved, then pour into a jug and leave to cool. When the syrup is cold, store it in the refrigerator until it is needed.

LEFT, Cider cup; RIGHT, Mulled wine

EGGNOG

SERVES 10–12
12 large eggs, separated
450 g (1 lb) caster sugar
300 ml (½ pint) bourbon whisky
300 ml (½ pint) rum
450 ml (¾ pint) double cream
grated nutmeg

Preparation time: 15 minutes plus chilling

An extremely filling concoction, this drink really takes the place of a meal.
1. Put the egg yolks in a bowl and beat in the sugar. When very smooth and creamy, beat in the bourbon and rum, little by little. Then gradually beat in the cream. Put in the refrigerator for 2–3 hours.
2. Beat the egg whites until stiff, and fold into the mixture.
3. Serve in glass bowls or short tumblers sprinkled with grated nutmeg.

SLOE GIN

MAKES ABOUT 6 BOTTLES
6 bottles dry gin
3 quarts sloes, washed
1.25 kg (2½ lb) lump sugar

Preparation time: about 2 hours

Sloes are ripe at the beginning of October, which is when this drink should be made. They are like a small bitter plum or damson, and can be found growing in profusion in wooded areas of southern England. This recipe makes a really excellent drink, far better than the commercially made one, ideal for Christmas drinking or to give as presents. Sloe gin is extremely strong and should be drunk in small glasses before meals, as an aperitif. You could make it up in half the quantities given for this recipe.

1. Half fill one huge earthenware crock or jar – capacity 2 gallons – or two smaller ones with the gin. Stick the head of a strong darning or embroidery needle into a cork, and prick each sloe two or three times. Drop them into the crock, add the sugar, and close the jar.
2. Leave for 2½–3 months – it will be just ready in time to bottle for Christmas – shaking the crock twice a week, or turning it on its side and rolling it over. The sloe gin is then ready to put into bottles.

CLARET CUP

SERVES 10–12
175 ml (6 fl oz) sugar syrup (see page 106)
175 ml (6 fl oz) lemon juice
450 ml (¾ pint) orange juice
85 ml (3 fl oz) orange curaçao
85 ml (3 fl oz) brandy
2 bottles red wine
6 long strips cucumber peel
ice cubes
1 l (1¾ pint) fizzy mineral water

Preparation time: about 15 minutes, plus standing and chilling

1. Find a largish jug that will fit in your refrigerator and, some hours before serving, mix the sugar syrup with the fruit juices. Add the spirits and wine, and put in the cucumber peel. Leave for an hour, then put in the refrigerator for another 2 hours.
2. Just before serving, add ice and the fizzy water. (Soda water can be used, but carbonated mineral water is much better.)

FROM THE LEFT: Egg nog, Sloe gin, Claret cup

MONACO

SERVES 1

dash of grenadine
ice cubes
light lager
fizzy lemonade

Preparation time: about 2 minutes

This delicious and virtually non-alcoholic cocktail is quickly and easily made.
1. Put a dash of grenadine into a tall glass. Add several ice cubes and fill up with equal parts of lager and fizzy lemonade. Mix lightly and serve immediately.

LEMONADE

SERVES 4–6

3 lemons, washed
3 tablespoons caster sugar
1.2 litres (2 pints) water

Preparation time: 10 minutes plus chilling

1. Cut the lemons in quarters, then cut each quarter in half to make eight pieces. Put them in a food processor or blender with the sugar and water. Process briefly, just until the lemons are roughly chopped, then pour through a strainer into a large jug. Alternatively, chop the lemons by hand.
2. Chill in the refrigerator and serve with ice.

Variation: For a mixed orange-and-lemonade, use 2 oranges, 2 lemons, and 2 tablespoons caster sugar.

GINGER ALE CUP

SERVES 4–6

65 ml (2½ fl oz) sugar syrup (see page 106)
65 ml (2½ fl oz) lemon juice
150 ml (¼ pint) orange juice
65 ml (2½ fl oz) ginger wine
4 strips cucumber peel
ice cubes
500 ml (18 fl oz) bottles ginger ale

To garnish:
½ orange, sliced
½ lemon, sliced

Preparation time: about 15 minutes, plus chilling

This is a delicious cup with practically no alcoholic content. It can easily be made in double quantities, or even more.
1. Mix the sugar syrup, the fruit juices and the ginger wine in a large jug and chill in the refrigerator. Add the cucumber peel. Have the ginger ale also chilling.
2. At the last moment, put lots of ice cubes in the jug, pour over the ginger ale and garnish with the sliced fruit.

FROM THE LEFT: Monaco, Lemonade, Ginger ale cup

PRESENTS TO MAKE

Here are presents with a deliciously personal touch: a mouth-watering assortment of gifts to make at home, ranging from tangy pickles and richly flavoured preserved fruits
to sweet and dainty biscuits
and confectionery.

MIXED DILL PICKLES

MAKES 5 × 450 g (1 lb) JARS
1 small cauliflower
225 g (8 oz) carrots
225 g (8 oz) string beans
100 g (4 oz) pickling onions, peeled
½ cucumber, unpeeled

Pickling mixture:
1.2 litres (2 pints) water
300 ml (½ pint) white wine vinegar
2 tablespoons pickling spice
25 g (1 oz) sea salt
50 g (2 oz) sugar
2 cloves garlic, peeled
1 tablespoon grated fresh horseradish
1 slice root ginger
1 stalk fresh dill, about 30 cm (12 inch) with
  flowerhead and seeds or 1 teaspoon dill
  seed
1 sprig fresh tarragon

Preparation time: about 40 minutes
plus cooling and maturing for at least
2 weeks
Cooking time: about 1 hour

The pickling mixture in this recipe can be used to preserve other vegetables, such as gherkins, pickling onions and cauliflower on their own.
1. Put all the ingredients for the pickling mixture in a saucepan and boil for 30 minutes. Leave to cool.
2. Wash the cauliflower and divide it into florets. Clean the carrots and cut them into quarters lengthwise, then into chunks. Cut the beans into 2.5 cm (1 inch) pieces.
3. Cook the cauliflower, carrots, beans and onions separately in a saucepan of lightly salted water, using the same water for each vegetable. Meanwhile, cut the unpeeled cucumber into quarters lengthwise, then into chunks. Drain the vegetables, discarding the cooking liquid, mix them with the cucumber and pack in jars.

4. Pour over the cooled pickling mixture through a sieve, removing the dill, tarragon, ginger and garlic (though fresh dill and tarragon added at this stage make the jars look pretty). Seal the jars and keep for 2 weeks before eating.

PICKLED CARROTS

For Pickled carrots, use 1 kg (2 lb) of baby carrots and the pickling mixture and method used for Mixed dill pickles. Wash and trim the carrots, retaining any trimmed green tops.

LEFT AND RIGHT: Mixed dill pickles; FRONT: Pickled carrots

TOMATO CHUTNEY

MAKES 3 × 450 g (1 lb) JARS
1.5 kg (3 lb) tomatoes, skinned and chopped
225 g (8 oz) eating apples, peeled, cored and
chopped
225 g (8 oz) onions, peeled and chopped
100 g (4 oz) raisins or sultanas
1 tablespoon salt
1 teaspoon black pepper
450 g (1 lb) soft brown sugar
1 teaspoon mustard seed, or ½ teaspoon
ground mustard powder
1 teaspoon ground allspice
900 ml (1½ pints) cider vinegar

Preparation time: about 40 minutes, plus
maturing for at least 2 weeks
Cooking time: about 1½ hours

1. Put the tomatoes, apples and onions into a preserving pan or a broad saucepan with a thick bottom. Add the raisins (or sultanas) and scatter the salt, pepper, brown sugar, mustard seed (or powder), and allspice over them. Pour on the vinegar.
2. Put over a gentle heat and bring slowly to the boil. Simmer gently, uncovered, until the mixture is thick and jammy. This will probably take about 1½ hours. It must be watched carefully, stirring every now and then, and skimming off the scum from the surface.
3. When the chutney is good and thick, remove from the stove and spoon it into hot sterilised jars. Wipe off any drips with a hot damp cloth. Leave to cool, then cover closely and store in a cool dark cupboard. Keep for 2 weeks before eating. Serve with bread and cheese, or cold meat.

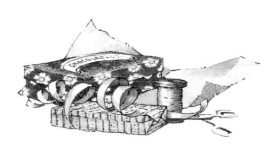

SALTED ALMONDS

whole almonds, blanched and peeled
butter
sea salt
cayenne pepper (optional)

Preparation time: 2–10 minutes
Cooking time: 3–4 minutes

I am not suggesting quantities here, since only you can know how many you will need; remember they are very more-ish! The almonds are best eaten the day they are made, but can be kept well for a few days if stored in air-tight containers, or carefully sealed into little packets of aluminium foil.

1. If the almonds are not already blanched, this is easily done. Put them in a bowl and pour over boiling water to cover. After a minute or two, take them out, a few at a time, and rub off the skins between the fingers. Dry them thoroughly in a cloth and they are ready for salting.

2. Heat some butter (allow 25 g/1 oz butter per 225 g/8 oz almonds) in a frying pan and when it is very hot, put in the almonds. Fry them quickly, turning frequently, until they are a pale golden – more of a straw colour than a brown – on both sides. Drain very well indeed on absorbent kitchen paper, then lay them on a plate and sprinkle with salt. Some people add cayenne pepper as well, but I prefer them without.

LEFT, Tomato chutney; RIGHT, Salted almonds

PRUNES IN WINE

prunes
red wine

Preparation time: depends on how many prunes you have to stone! Leave to mature for 10 days.

Another recipe for you to decide how much to make. To make the prunes even more of a delicious treat, fill each prune with a whole, unpeeled almond before packing it into the jar.

1. Take the best quality prunes, remove the stones carefully, and pack into a small glass jar with a well-fitting lid. Fill up the jar with a good red wine. Close the jar securely and leave for 10 days.

2. Serve from the jar, with a fork to get them out, with coffee at the end of a meal.

PEACHES IN BRANDY

MAKES 2 × 450 g (1 lb) JARS
300 ml (½ pint) water
225 g (8 oz) lump or granulated sugar
1 piece cinnamon stick
4 cloves
4 peaches, white-fleshed if possible
4 tablespoons brandy

Preparation time: 15 minutes plus cooling overnight and maturing for at least a week
Cooking time: 7 minutes, plus making the syrup

These make a nice present, or a delicious treat to serve to friends. Accompany them with a crème brûlée, a cold creamy rice pudding, or a crème caramel.

1. Make a syrup by boiling the water with the sugar, cinnamon and cloves.
2. When the sugar has melted, put in the peaches, cut in half and with the stones removed. After 3 minutes, lift them out and skin them. (If totally ripe, they may be skinned before poaching.) Return the peaches to the syrup and poach for another 4 minutes. Leave them to cool in the syrup.

3. The next day, lift out the peaches and put them into a glass jar. Boil up the syrup till slightly reduced, mix with the brandy and pour over the peaches, removing the cinnamon and cloves. Leave to cool, then close the jar tightly. Do not eat for a week or two.

APRICOTS IN WHITE WINE

MAKES 1 × 450 g (1 lb) JAR
225 g (8 oz) dried apricots
250–300 ml (8–10 fl oz) sweetish white wine

Preparation time: 10 minutes, plus maturing for at least a week

These are delicious eaten at the end of a meal, with coffee. A narrow fork is useful for fishing them out of the jar.

1. Take the best dried apricots you can find and wash them carefully.
2. Pack loosely into jars and cover with a fairly sweet, but good, white wine such as Vouvray Demi-sec. A few whole blanched almonds could be added to the jar, if you like.
3. Screw the lids on tightly and leave for a week before eating.

LEFT TO RIGHT: Prunes in wine, Peaches in brandy, Apricots in white wine

GINGER THINS

MAKES ABOUT 24

100 g (4 oz) plain flour
¾ teaspoon ground ginger
100 g (4 oz) butter, cut in bits
100 g (4 oz) light brown sugar
1 heaped tablespoon golden syrup
1 heaped tablespoon treacle
2 tablespoons whipping cream

Preparation time: 15 minutes
Cooking time: about 20 minutes
Oven: 180°C, 350°F, Gas Mark 4

These are delicious biscuits, crisp and lacy thin, for eating with fruit salad, ice cream, or compotes of fruit. They are best eaten the same day, but the dough can be made 1–2 days in advance and kept in the refrigerator, or frozen. Be sure to bring it back to room temperature before using.

1. Sift the flour into a large bowl with the ginger. Rub in first the butter, then the brown sugar. Warm the syrup and treacle together with the cream, then stir into the dry ingredients. Mix well, beating with a wooden spoon.

2. Using a large teaspoon, drop the ginger mixture on to baking sheets, leaving about a 6 cm (2½ inch) space between each biscuit. You may fill up to 3 baking sheets. Bake in a preheated oven for about 10 minutes per baking sheet or until they are cooked in the centre and lightly coloured around the edges.

3. Take the baking sheet out of the oven and leave for 2–3 minutes, then lift the biscuits carefully with a palette knife. Lay them either on a flat surface, or, if you prefer curved biscuits, over a greased rolling pin, or glass bottle. They will become crisp on cooling.

SPICED CHRISTMAS COOKIES

MAKES 24 COOKIES

120 g (4½ oz) unsalted butter, at room
*   temperature*
75 g (3 oz) soft brown sugar
150 g (5 oz) plain flour, sifted
1 teaspoon ground cinnamon
¼ teaspoon ground cloves
¼ teaspoon grated or ground nutmeg
¼ teaspoon grated or ground ginger
1 egg, beaten

Preparation time: 25 minutes plus chilling
Cooking time: 10–12 minutes
Oven: 180°C, 350°F, Gas Mark 4

1. Cream together the butter and the brown sugar until light and fluffy, then add the sifted flour and spices and mix well.

2. Stir in the beaten egg and mix well, forming a ball.

3. Turn the mixture out and wrap in cling film; chill in the refrigerator for several hours to firm up.

4. Roll out to about 5 mm (¼ inch) thick and cut into star shapes with a floured cutter.

5. Lift the cookies carefully with a palette knife, and lay on oiled baking sheets. Gather up any scraps, put briefly in the freezer or ice compartment, then roll them out again to the same thickness as before and cut out more cookies.

6. If you think you may like to hang the cookies on the Christmas tree, use a skewer to make holes for ribbon at this stage.

7. Bake for 10–12 minutes in a preheated moderate oven.

8. Allow the biscuits to cool slightly before lifting off the baking sheet. Keep in an airtight tin.

LEFT, Ginger thins; RIGHT, Spiced Christmas cookies

PEPPERMINT CREAMS

MAKES ABOUT 36 CREAMS
450 g (1 lb) icing sugar
2 small egg whites
5–6 drops essence of peppermint

Preparation time: about 30 minutes plus drying overnight

Unlike most sweets, these are easy and safe for children to make, since they do not require any cooking. They are useful as a last-minute present, wrapped in cellophane and tied with ribbon, or as a sweetmeat to serve with coffee. They look pretty piled in small glass dishes on the table.

1. Sift the icing sugar into a large bowl. Beat the egg whites until they foam, but are not yet thick. Stir them into the sugar, beating with a wooden spoon until they form a cohesive mass. Continue to beat until the texture changes, and becomes smooth and glossy.
2. Now add the peppermint essence, tasting as you do so, stopping when the flavour is right.

3. Sift a little more icing sugar on to a flat surface and lay the mixture on it. Roll out until it is about 1 cm (½ inch) thick. If you have a small round cutter about 2.5 cm (1 inch) wide, you can use this to cut out the sweets. Aspic cutters could also be used to vary the shapes. Otherwise take teaspoonfuls of the mixture and roll between the hands to make more-or-less round shapes.
4. Lay them on a sheet of foil to dry. Turn them over after a few hours, then leave till the following day. Store in an airtight tin.

TABLET

MAKES ABOUT 24 SQUARES
butter, for greasing
450 g (1 lb) granulated sugar
150 ml (¼ pint) single cream
a pinch of salt
¼ teaspoon vanilla essence

Preparation time: 15 minutes plus cooling
Cooking time: 20–25 minutes

This is a delicious vanilla-flavoured fudge which we used to eat at Christmas time when we were children in Scotland. It is easier to make than toffee, and is useful for small presents, wrapped in cellophane and tied with a scarlet ribbon.

1. Choose a tin measuring 13 or 15 cm square × 4 cm deep (5 or 6 inches × 1½ inches) and rub it with butter.
2. Put the sugar in a fairly large heavy-bottomed saucepan, adding the cream and a pinch of salt. Heat over a low heat, stirring steadily for several minutes until the sugar has melted. Then raise the heat to moderate, cease stirring, and let it boil steadily until it reaches 118°C/245°F or 'soft-ball' stage. If you don't have a sugar thermometer, test it by dropping a small drop into a cup of cold water. If hot enough, it will immediately become a firm ball.

3. Once this stage has been reached, remove the pan from the heat and beat well. When the bubbles have stopped forming, stir in the vanilla essence and continue to beat until it thickens, scraping the sides and bottom of the pan. (You can speed up this stage by standing the pan in a sink half full of cold water.)
4. When smooth and creamy, but still runny enough to pour, tip it into the greased tin as smoothly as you can. If it has become too thick to pour, you can warm it a little and try again.
5. When cool, mark into small squares. When completely cold, break it into the marked squares, and wrap in cellophane or foil.

CLOKWISE FROM TOP LEFT: Peppermint creams, Candied fruit in chocolate (see page 124), Grapes in chocolate (see page 124), Tablet

CANDIED FRUIT IN CHOCOLATE

MAKES ABOUT 60 PIECES

candied orange and lemon slices, or candied strips of ginger, or candied strips of orange or lemon peel
90–100 g (3½–4 oz) plain chocolate
½ teaspoon safflower oil

Preparation time: about 25 minutes plus cooling and setting

Illustrated on page 123

Making your own candied fruit is quite a production, and it is not one that I am prepared to undertake, just before Christmas. Better by far, buy the candied fruit and dip it in chocolate, which is extremely easy, and very effective.
1. Melt the chocolate and oil together, as for Grapes in chocolate (see below). Then dip the pieces of fruit, or ginger, in the chocolate until they are two-thirds covered.
2. Lay them on foil, shiny side up, until the chocolate has cooled and set. Then lift carefully, peeling off the foil, and lay in a glass dish if using as table decorations, or wrap in cellophane for presents.

GRAPES IN CHOCOLATE

a large bunch of white grapes
100 g (4 oz) plain chocolate
½ teaspoon safflower oil

Preparation time: about 25 minutes plus cooling and setting

Illustrated on page 123

These grapes dipped in chocolate make a pretty table decoration, but are rather fragile to wrap as presents. It is important to use a good quality dark chocolate. The amount of chocolate suggested here should be sufficient to coat 60 grapes.
1. Using scissors, cut each grape singly, leaving a short stalk to hold it by.
2. Break the chocolate in a bowl standing over a pan of very hot water. Heat gently, without allowing it to boil. As it melts, add the oil. When melted and smooth, dip in the grapes one at a time, holding them by their stalks, so that they are two-thirds covered with chocolate.
3. Lay the grapes on a sheet of foil (shiny side up) to cool. When they are cold lift them very carefully and lay them in a pretty dish.

$\mathcal{F}$OOD FACTS

HELEN DORE

CHRISTMAS COOKING

A time for giving and a time for sharing, Christmas is the season of joy, good will and good cheer. While all cooks know the pleasure good food gives, and never more so than at Christmas, they also know that great demands will be made on their time.

This chapter guides the home cook through the maze of preparations and day-to-day cooking inseparable from a family Christmas. There are sections on preparing the great traditional foods of Christmas and on cooking less traditional foods as well. Advance planning is made easier by the lists and notes on buying in advance and storing foods and drinks, and there is a detailed count-down to take the cook through Christmas Eve and Christmas Day.

THE CHRISTMAS BIRD

For many people, Christmas dinner just wouldn't be the same without a splendid roast turkey with all the trimmings dominating the dining table. Full instructions on choosing and cooking the Christmas turkey, with ideas for stuffings and accompaniments, can be found on pages 130–1, and more recipes can be found in the first two chapters in this book.

However, turkey is a relative newcomer to the Christmas scene in this country, being unknown in Europe before the New World was discovered late in the 15th century, and in days gone by a roast goose featured on most Christmas menus. This can be a delicious alternative to turkey, the richness and fine flavour of the meat making it a very festive choice. A sharp, subtly spiced apple sauce makes a perfect accompaniment to goose, as in the recipe on page 46, or you might like to try an apple and prune stuffing (see recipe). Lightly fried apple rings would make an attractive garnish, or peeled, cored, halved dessert apples poached in a light sugar syrup then filled with cranberry sauce or redcurrant jelly and arranged round the goose.

Turkey and goose are ideal birds for Christmas as they will feed a large number of people. Goose especially, is also a rich meat so that people tend to eat smaller portions. For smaller parties – 4, say, or even 2 – excellent alternatives would be roast pheasant served with traditional game chips, fried breadcrumbs and a root vegetable purée, or roast duck stuffed with sage and onion and served with a piquant apple sauce.

APPLE AND PRUNE STUFFING
225 g (8 oz) fresh white breadcrumbs
175 g (6 oz) prunes, soaked, stoned and chopped
350 g (12 oz) cooking apples, peeled, cored and chopped
30 ml (2 tablespoons) chopped parsley
75 g (3 oz) butter
1 large onion, peeled and finely chopped
finely grated rind and juice of 1 lemon
1 egg, lightly beaten
salt and black pepper

1. Place the breadcrumbs in a bowl with the prunes, apples and parsley. Melt the butter in a small pan, add the onion and fry gently until softened but not coloured.
2. Add to the breadcrumb mixture, then stir in the lemon rind and juice and egg to bind. Season to taste with salt and pepper.

THE CHRISTMAS CAKE

A rich fruit cake, made well in advance and liberally dosed with injections of brandy over a number of weeks, then marzipanned and iced as described on pages 132–136, is a natural centrepiece for the Christmas tea table. It's fun to experiment with different shapes and sizes – and there are endless ideas for decoration, from simple ornaments to elaborate icing creations.

If you prefer an un-iced cake, a topping of prettily arranged blanched almonds or Brazil nuts and glacé fruits looks most festive and attractive. Christmas cake stores so well in a tin that it will last throughout the Christmas season and beyond – in fact, it will probably prove most popular after the Day itself, when people have usually eaten too much dinner to appreciate it fully.

THE CHRISTMAS PUDDING

Plum pudding, topped with a sprig of holly and brought flaming to the table in a shimmering blue haze of alcohol, is a splendidly dramatic conclusion to Christmas dinner. You could give your Christmas meal a very smart touch by making individual Christmas puddings. Brandy butter (see page 9) is the traditional accompaniment to Christmas pudding, but it can be fun to ring the changes, substituting rum for brandy, or cointreau to give a delicious orange-flavoured butter. Whipped cream, well laced with brandy, or a liqueur such as drambuie, is also delicious with the pudding, as is a creamy custard sauce. Should you have any Christmas pudding left over, you can make this into a wonderful ice cream, which can be stored in the freezer and brought out for a New Year dinner party (see recipe, right).

For those who may find the traditional pudding served with Brandy butter rather overpowering at the end of a big meal, there are deliciously light alternatives: seasonal Cranberry kissel, for instance (see recipe, right), or a bowl of caramelized oranges or exotic fruit salad (see page 66) or a traditional English trifle (page 102) or prettily moulded fresh fruit jelly.

CHRISTMAS PUDDING ICE CREAM
SERVES 4–6

4 eggs, separated
100 g (4 oz) caster sugar
100–175 g (4–6 oz) left-over Christmas pudding
2 tablespoons rum
300 ml (½ pint) double cream

1. Whisk the egg yolks with the sugar until thick and pale. Break up the Christmas pudding with a fork and distribute it evenly through the yolk mixture. Stir in the rum.
2. Whip the cream until it forms soft peaks and fold into the mixture, followed by the stiffly whisked egg whites. Freeze in the refrigerator for several hours until set. (This ice cream does not require beating during freezing.)

CRANBERRY KISSEL
SERVES 6–8

350 g (12 oz) cranberries
1.2 l (2 pints) water
450 g (1 lb) sugar
3 tablespoons potato flour, dissolved in 300 ml (½ pint) cold water

1. Place the cranberries in a pan with 600 ml (1 pint) water, bring to the boil, then simmer for about 5 minutes, until they start to burst. Remove from the heat and cool slightly, then purée in a blender or food processor until quite smooth.
2. Press the cranberry purée through a sieve, reserve the juice and return the debris in the sieve to a pan, with the remaining water. Bring to the boil and boil for 5 minutes, then strain into a clean pan, add the sugar and bring to the boil.
3. Add the potato flour mixture to the pan and return to the boil, stirring continuously. Stir in the reserved cranberry juice and strain if lumpy.
4. Pour the kissel into pretty serving glasses and serve chilled.

Other countries make very attractive Christmas cakes too and you might like to sample some of these for a change. Italian *panettone* is a very light yeast cake, either plain or lightly fruited and served sprinkled with a powdery frosting of icing sugar. It is sold in this country at Christmas time in specialist Italian food stores, Italian restaurants and some super markets. The spiced fruit bread on page

16 is not only good for tea but makes a very acceptable accompaniment to a glass of wine. For those who do not care for rich fruit cake, it also makes an acceptable Christmas cake.

From Germany, Stöllen is another delicious Christmas yeast fruit cake, shaped like a log, with an irresistible marzipan filling. Stöllen is now available in this country from many supermarkets.

French Bûche de Noel, or Yuletide Log, is more of a dessert than a cake and is becoming increasingly popular in this country. An attractive Christmas Log cake, popular with children, can be easily made from a Swiss roll filled with chocolate buttercream or a more 'Christmasy' mixture of sweetened chestnut purée and cream, then coated with a chocolate buttercream icing.

ADVANCE SHOPPING

At Christmas there are more demands on the cook than at any other time of year. However, it need not be a daunting experience; sensible advance planning will ensure you enjoy it just as much as everyone else!

As soon as your Christmas catering plans have been finalized and a menu roughed out, draw up a shopping list, dividing it into store-cupboard and freezer items which can be bought well in advance when the shops are not so crowded, and perishable items, which need to be bought nearer the time.

STORE CUPBOARD

Dried pulses: a good supply of these is invaluable for soups and casseroles, which make excellent family fare between the festive meals. Include some of the quicker-cooking pulses, like split peas.

Canned pulses: a selection of red kidney beans, green flageolets, butter beans, chick peas, etc. is very useful for salads and dips.

Dried pasta: make sure you have spaghetti in stock and one or two interesting shapes like bows or shells: a steaming bowl of pasta can make a very welcome change from rich food.

Canned chestnut purée: excellent for stuffings. The sweetened variety makes a wonderful instant dessert, whipped up with cream, or a filling for Christmas log cake.

Olives: canned or bottled olives – include some stuffed ones, and the small black Greek olives, which have a specially good flavour – are an extremely useful store-cupboard item, for serving with Christmas drinks, or garnishing.

Nuts: assorted salted nuts, in tins or packets, are always popular as cocktail nibbles. Unsalted nuts, particularly blanched almonds, Brazils, hazelnuts and walnuts, are useful for savoury dishes like soups and salads, and for decorating desserts. A bowl of mixed nuts in their shells – make sure you've got a nutcracker! – looks very attractive on the Christmas table. Don't forget ground almonds for almond paste.

Savoury biscuits and crackers: you will need plenty of these, for serving with cheese, or as the base of cocktail canapés.

Mincemeat: you'll probably be making your own (see recipe, page 20), but a jar or two is always handy for emergency mince pies or a lattice tart.

Dried and glacé fruit: you will need a good supply of these for puddings and cakes.

Drinks: lay in Christmas wines and spirits, and don't forget plenty of mineral water, mixers and fruit juice and squash.

PERISHABLE FOODS

Storage can be a problem for these, as refrigerator space always seems to be quite inadequate at Christmas. However, many perishable foods, especially vegetables, can be successfully stored, provided they are carefully wrapped and protected, in a cold, dry place away from centrally heated rooms.

	STORAGE
Fresh turkey	2–3 days in refrigerator
Fresh goose	2–3 days in refrigerator
Fresh duck	2–3 days in refrigerator
Fresh beef	2–3 days in refrigerator
Ham (fresh)	10 days in refrigerator
Ham (vacuum-packed)	3 weeks in refrigerator
Bacon rashers	1 week in refrigerator
Cocktail sausages	3–4 days in refrigerator
Smoked salmon (vacuum-packed)	1 week in refrigerator
Cream (buy cartons with replaceable plastic lid)	up to 1 week; check sell-by date carefully
Butter	several weeks in refrigerator; depends on sell-by date
Cheese (wrap in foil)	up to 1 week in cold place or refrigerator, but always serve at room temperature
Salad vegetables	2–3 days in refrigerator salad compartment
Root vegetables such as potatoes, carrots, parsnips	2 weeks in cold dry place
Onions	2–3 weeks in cold dry place
Apples	several weeks in cold dry place
Pears	about 1 week, depending on ripeness, in cold dry place
Citrus fruit	up to 2 weeks in cold dry place
Exotic fruit	3–4 days in cold dry place

FREEZER

Depending on the capacity of your freezer, all the following foods could be usefully bought in advance and kept on ice for Christmas:

FREEZER LIFE

Turkey	6 months
Goose	4 months
Duck	6 months
Beef joint	8 months
Bacon joint (smoked)	6 weeks
Bacon rashers (smoked)	6–8 weeks
Smoked salmon	6 months
Vegetables such as Brussels sprouts,	
petits pois, broccoli spears	12 months
Cranberries and other soft fruit	12 months
Butter (unsalted)	6 months
Butter (salted)	3 months
Cream	3 months
Pastry (unbaked)	3 months
Bread (baked)	6 months

FREEZER CHRISTMAS COOKING

Make optimum use of your freezer, not only to store ready-frozen ingredients but also to stock up with many of the dishes, either fully or partially cooked, which you'll be serving over Christmas. Any of the following make invaluable additions to the freezer, as from the beginning of November:

Soups, stocks and sauces
Pâtés
Casseroles
Vegetable purées
Chopped herbs
Breadcrumbs and stuffings
Mincemeat
Pastry cases (baked or unbaked)
Mince pies (baked or unbaked)
Pancakes
Sponge cake for trifle
Ice cream and sorbet

CHRISTMAS COUNTDOWN

Cooking for Christmas can usefully begin as far as 3 months in advance.
October: make chutney and sloe gin, pickle onions, bottle fruit.
November: make puddings and cake. Start cooking for freezer (see below).

December: ice and decorate the Christmas cake. About 1 week before Christmas, make stuffings, mayonnaise and salad dressings and store well covered in refrigerator. Start thawing a large frozen turkey the day before Christmas Eve.

COOKING THE CHRISTMAS DINNER

There will be no panics if you start the preparations on Christmas Eve, enlist some helpers to peel and trim vegetables, etc., and follow a carefully timed schedule.

CHRISTMAS EVE
- Thaw turkey if frozen (see thawing times for turkey, page 130).
- As soon as giblets can be removed, use to make stock for gravy.
- Remove soup, sauces, brandy butter, etc. from freezer and leave to thaw.
- Prick sausages for turkey garnish.
- Peel, parboil and drain potatoes for roasting.
- Trim but do not wash Brussels sprouts.

ON THE DAY
The following schedule is drawn up to serve lunch at 1 p.m., cooking a 4.5 kg (10 lb) turkey (see page 131 for turkey cooking times):
8.30 a.m. Pre-heat oven.
Stuff, truss and bard turkey.
9 Put turkey in to cook, and remember to baste it every 20 minutes or so.
Remove mince pies from freezer, if serving.
Finish any cold desserts you may be serving, e.g. cream topping for trifle.
10 Put Christmas pudding on to steam.
Lay table.
Uncork red wine and make sure white wine is chilling.
11.30 Heat dripping for roast potatoes and put to roast, together with sausages and bacon rolls for turkey.
Bring cheese, if serving, to room temperature.
12 Put plates, serving dishes and rolls to accompany soup to warm.
12.30 Put sprouts on to cook.
Heat soup.
Turn out pudding and keep warm.
12.40 Remove turkey from oven. Check that it is cooked through, then leave to stand while making gravy.
12.50 Drain and dish up vegetables. Keep warm in oven.
Garnish turkey and keep warm while serving soup.
Put mince pies in oven while serving main course.

THE CHRISTMAS TURKEY

Few people nowadays buy a really huge turkey at Christmas such as Mr Pickwick tucked into at Dingley Dell. It is a good idea to buy a relatively small bird and eat off it twice, once hot and once cold, using the remains to make a good soup.

A complete recipe for roasting a turkey can be found on page 28, as part of the traditional Christmas lunch menu. Here you will find some useful facts, figures and tips to help you make the most of your turkey.

BUYING AND PREPARING THE BIRD

Turkey is the most popular choice of Christmas poultry because unlike goose and duck, which are at their best hot, it is equally good hot or cold, and can feed a crowd.

Here is a rough guide to help you work out the correct weight of turkey to buy:

Oven-ready Weight	Servings
2.75–3.5 kg (6–8 lb)	6–10
4.5–6 kg (10–13 lb)	12–20
6.5–9 kg (14–20 lb)	20–30

A 4.5 kg (10 lb) bird will yield about 2.4 kg (5 lb 8 oz) meat. It would serve 8 people as a hot meal, with enough for seconds, plus a further 4–6 servings as cold cuts.

Whatever the weight of turkey you decide on, do make sure that it is the right size for your oven! If you are planning to feed a great many people over Christmas, you might find it easier to buy two smaller birds and cook one in advance to keep for a Boxing Day buffet, for example.

Fresh or Frozen?
The big advantage of a frozen bird is that it can be kept in the freezer, leaving you free of that nagging worry that you may not get to the shops before stocks run out! You may like to buy one of the self-basting, 'butter-ball' birds, which yield specially moist, succulent meat. Frozen turkey needs very careful thawing (see below) and once thawed must on no account be re-frozen.

Many people prefer to buy a fresh turkey, in which case it is highly advisable to order it in advance, and of course you must make sure that you have room to store it in the refrigerator or other place at a temperature of no more than 40°F.

Thawing Frozen Turkey
It is most important that turkey should be thoroughly thawed in its bag, and the liquid drained off as it is exuded. Take a small turkey out of the freezer early on Christmas Eve, or on 23 December if it is a large bird (over 6.8 kg/15 lb). *Do not thaw in the refrigerator.*

At room temperature

Oven-ready Weight	Thawing Time
2.75–3.5 kg (6–8 lb)	16 hours
4.5 kg (10 lb)	18 hours
6.8 kg (15 lb)	24 hours
9 kg (20 lb)	30 hours

In the Microwave
The freezer bag must be pierced and the metal tag removed before placing the turkey in the microwave. Allow 10–12 minutes per 450 g (1 lb) on LOW, then drain off any liquid and stand the bird, still in its bag, in cold water for 2–3 hours.

STUFFING A TURKEY

Allow about 225 g (8 oz) stuffing per 2.25 kg (5 lb) turkey (oven-ready weight). Stuff the bird at the neck end only just before cooking. Do not pack the stuffing too tightly, and do not stuff the vent end, or the bird will not cook properly in the calculated time (see below). Any left-over stuffing can be shaped into small balls and cooked separately, either in the oven along with the turkey or shallow fried, then used to garnish the bird.

Chestnut stuffing (see page 13) is traditional with turkey, but it can be fun to try out some other ideas. Cranberries make a delicious stuffing (see the recipe below), or there are other suggestions on page 16.

CRANBERRY STUFFING
100 g (4 oz) caster sugar
125 ml (14 fl oz) water
225 g (8 oz) cranberries
100 g (4 oz) fresh white breadcrumbs
50 g (2 oz) seedless raisins
finely grated rind of 1 orange
1 teaspoon salt
freshly ground black pepper
¼ teaspoon cinnamon
50 g (2 oz) butter, melted

1. Dissolve the sugar in the water in a small saucepan. Add the cranberries and bring to the boil, then simmer for 5–10 minutes, until the berries pop.
2. Meanwhile combine all the remaining ingredients in a bowl. Add the cranberries with their juice and mix thoroughly to combine.

COOKING THE TURKEY

Roasting a Turkey

The cooking time must be calculated on the stuffed weight. Allow 20 minutes per 450 g (1 lb) plus 20 minutes, then 15–30 minutes standing time, to facilitate carving.

Turkey meat can be rather dry, so brush all over with melted butter, and cover the breast with rashers of streaky bacon. Baste the turkey several times during cooking. Cover the breast with foil towards the end of roasting time if it shows signs of over-browning.

Microwaving a Turkey

Turkey can be cooked in half the conventional time in a microwave oven. Allow 9–11 minutes on HIGH per 450 g (1 lb), plus 15–30 minutes standing time.

Mask the wings and legs with tiny pieces of foil. Stand the turkey breast side down on a microware roasting rack or inverted plate in a shallow dish (or the turkey may be cooked in a roasting bag).

Halfway through cooking, turn the bird, brush all over with a glaze (see recipes), then complete cooking.

MICROWAVED TURKEY GLAZES

50 g (2 oz) butter
2 tablespoons soft dark brown sugar
2 teaspoons sherry
2 teaspoons soy sauce
or
50 g (2 oz) butter
3 tablespoons cranberry sauce
1 tablespoons port

1. Heat the ingredients gently in a small pan until dissolved, then use a pastry brush to brush over the turkey.

TURKEY LEFT-OVERS

Cold turkey makes a delicious meal in itself with a selection of salads, jacket potatoes and a tangy Cumberland sauce (see below).

CUMBERLAND SAUCE

1 small onion, peeled and minced
2 oranges
1 lemon
225 g (8 oz) redcurrant jelly
5 ml (1 tsp) Dijon mustard
150 ml (¼ pint) port
2 tablespoons arrowroot
salt
freshly ground black pepper

1. Put the onion in a small saucepan. Thinly pare the rind of one of the oranges and the lemon, cut it into thin strips and add to the pan. Cover with cold water, bring to the boil, then simmer for 5 minutes. Drain.
2. Melt the redcurrant jelly in a saucepan.

Stir in the juice of both oranges and the lemon, the mustard, port and the blanched onion and citrus rind. Simmer gently for 5 minutes.
3. Mix the arrowroot to a paste with 1 tablespoon of water and add to the mixture in the pan.
4. Season to taste and simmer without boiling for a further 2–3 minutes, then pour into a screwtop jar and leave to cool. Close tightly and keep for 1 week before using.

Cold turkey is also good in a pie or salad, and combined with a cheese sauce and topped with crumbs and grated cheese, makes a delicious gratin dish.

Small quantities of cooked turkey meat can be minced or finely chopped, mixed with a thick, creamy Béchamel sauce, and used to fill pancakes or vol au vents. Once the carcase has been stripped clean, it can be used to make a well-flavoured soup.

TURKEY AND CELERY SOUP

1 turkey carcase
1 onion, peeled and quartered
4 carrots, halved
1 bay leaf
50 g (2 oz) butter
2 onions, peeled and finely chopped
1 head celery, chopped
1 large potato, peeled and diced
salt and black pepper
150 ml (¼ pint) single cream

1. Break up the carcase and place in a large saucepan with the onion, carrots and bay leaf. Cover with cold water, bring to the boil and simmer for 1½ hours. Strain.
2. Melt the butter in a pan, add the onion, celery and potato and sweat gently for 5 minutes. Add the turkey stock, bring to the boil, then simmer for about 40 minutes or until the vegetables are tender.
3. Purée in a blender, season to taste and reheat. Before serving stir in the cream.

THE CHRISTMAS CAKE

The traditional plum cake recipe on p. 30 does not contain alcohol. The following recipe is made with brandy (it would also be good with sherry), and for an even more alcoholic result, and a very moist cake, the surface may be pricked and 2 tablespoons brandy poured over at 2-week intervals after baking, before the cake is marzipanned and iced as described on pages 134–6. The quantities given are for an 18-cm (7-inch) round cake, but the chart below will help you calculate quantities for different-sized round and square tins.

CHRISTMAS CAKE WITH BRANDY

For cake sizes and ingredients see chart opposite.

1. Grease and double-line the cake tin of your chosen size. Heat the oven to 150°C, 300°F, Gas Mark 2.
2. Place the dried fruit and mixed peel in a

mixing bowl and stir in the ground almonds.
3. Quarter, wash and dry the cherries. Add to the bowl with the citrus rinds.
4. In another mixing bowl, cream together the butter, sugar and treacle until light and fluffy.
5. Sift the flours with the cinnamon, mixed spice and nutmeg.

6. Beat the eggs into the creamed mixture one at a time, following each addition with 2 tablespoons of spiced flour. Fold in the remaining flour alternately with the brandy.
7. Mix in the dried fruit mixture evenly and turn into the prepared tin. Spread out evenly and smooth the surface.
8. Cut 6 strips of brown paper to measure the depth and circumference of the tin and tie round the outside of the tin to prevent the outside edge of the cake becoming tough or hard during baking.
9. Bake the cake just below the centre of the oven for 3 hours or until a skewer inserted into the centre comes out clean.
10. Remove from the oven and leave to cool in the tin for 10 minutes, then turn out on to a wire tray and leave to cool completely.
11. Do not remove the lining paper. Wrap the cake in foil and store in an airtight tin for up to 2 months; or freeze for up to 6 months.

12. To increase the brandy content of the cake, unwrap it once or twice during storage, prick the surface with a skewer and drizzle two tablespoons of brandy over the cake.

ROUND TIN:	13 cm (5 inch)
depth:	5 cm (2 inch)
weight:	625 g (1 lb 6 oz)
cooking time:	2¼ hours

SHALLOW SQUARE:	13 cm (5 inch)
depth:	4.75 (1⅞ inch)
weight:	625 g (1 lb 6 oz)
cooking time:	2¼ hours

DEEP SQUARE:	
depth:	
weight:	
cooking time:	

currants	100 g (4 oz)
sultanas	100 g (4 oz)
raisins	50 g (2 oz)
mixed peel	40 g (1½ oz)
ground almonds	15 g (½ oz)
glacé cherries	50 g (2 oz)
lemon rind	½ lemon
orange rind	½ orange
butter	65 g (2½ oz)
dark soft brown sugar	65 g (2½ oz)
eggs (size 1 or 2)	1
brandy	2 teaspoons
black treacle	1 teaspoon
self-raising flour	25 g (1 oz)
plain flour	50 g (2 oz)
ground cinnamon	¼ teaspoon
mixed spice	good pinch
ground nutmeg	pinch

15 cm (6 inch)	18 cm (7 inch)	20 cm (8 inch)	23 cm (9 inch)	25 cm (10 inch)	28 cm (11 inch)	30 cm (12 inch)
5.5 cm (2¼ inch)	6 cm (2½ inch)	6 cm (2½ inch)	6 cm (2½ inch)	7 cm (2¾ inch)	7 cm (2¾ inch)	7.5 cm (3 inch)
900 g (2 lb)	1.5 kg (3 lb)	1.75 kg (3¾ lb)	2.5 kg (5½ lb)	3.2 kg (7 lb 5 oz)	3.8 kg (8 lb 12 oz)	4.7 kg (10 lb 6 oz)
2¾ hours	3 hours	3½ hours	4 hours	4¾ hours	5 hours	5¼ hours

15 cm (6 inch)	18 cm (7 inch)	20 cm (8 inch)	23 cm (9 inch)	25 cm (10 inch)	28 cm (11 inch)	30 cm (12 inch)
5 cm (2 inch)	5.5 cm (2¼ inch)	5.5 cm (2¼ inch)	5.5 cm (2¼ inch)	5.6 cm (2¼ inch)	5.6 cm (2¼ inch)	6 cm (2½ inch)
900 g (2 lb)	1.5 kg (3 lb)	1.75 kg (3¾ lb)	2.5 kg (5½ lb)	3.2 kg (7 lb 5 oz)	3.8 kg (8 lb 12 oz)	4.7 kg (10 lb 6 oz)
2¼ hours	2¾ hours	3¼ hours	3¾ hours	4½ hours	4½ hours	5 hours

13 cm (5 inch)	15 cm (6 inch)	18 cm (7 inch)	20 cm (8 inch)	23 cm (9 inch)	25 cm (10 inch)	28 cm (11 inch)
7 cm (2¾ inch)	7 cm (2¾ inch)	7 cm (2¾ inch)	7.5 cm (3 inch)	7.5 cm (3 inch)	7.5 cm (3 inch)	7.5 cm (3 inch)
900 g (2 lb)	1.5 kg (3 lb)	1.75 kg (3¾ lb)	2.5 kg (5½ lb)	3.2 kg (7 lb 5 oz)	3.8 kg (8 lb 12 oz)	4.6 kg (10 lb 6 oz)
2½ hours	3 hours	3½ hours	4½ hours	5 hours	5½ hours	5½ hours

165 g (5½ oz)	215 g (7½ oz)	300 g (11 oz)	450 g (1 lb)	625 g (1 lb 6 oz)	725 g (1 lb 10 oz)	950 g (1 lb 4 oz)
165 g (5½ oz)	215 g (7½ oz)	300 g (11 oz)	450 g (1 lb)	625 g (1 lb 6 oz)	725 g (1 lb 10 oz)	950 g (1 lb 14 oz)
75 g (3 oz)	150 g (5 oz)	200 g (7 oz)	275 g (10 oz)	350 g (12 oz)	400 g (14 oz)	450 g (1 lb)
50 g (2 oz)	65 g (2½ oz)	75 g (3 oz)	100 g (4 oz)	175 g (6 oz)	225 g (8 oz)	250 g (9 oz)
25 g (1 oz)	40 g (1½ oz)	50 g (2 oz)	75 g (3 oz)	100 g (4 oz)	150 g (5 oz)	175 g (6 oz)
75 g (3 oz)	90 g (3½ oz)	100 g (4 oz)	175 g (6 oz)	225 g (8 oz)	275 g (10 oz)	300 g (11 oz)
½ lemon	1 lemon	1 lemon	1½ lemons	2 lemons	2 lemons	2 lemons
½ orange	½ orange	½ orange	1 orange	1 orange	1 orange	1 orange
90 g (3½ oz)	150 g (5 oz)	200 g (7 oz)	275 g (10 oz)	400 g (14 oz)	475 g (1 lb 1 oz)	550 g (1 lb 4 oz)
90 g (3½ oz)	150 g (5 oz)	200 g (7 oz)	275 g (10 oz)	400 g (14 oz)	475 g (1 lb 1 oz)	550 g (1 lb 4 oz)
2	3	4	5	6	7	9
1 tablespoon	2 tablespoons	3 tablespoons	4 tablespoons	4½ tablespoons	5 tablespoons	6 tablespoons
1 teaspoon	2 teaspoons	1 tablespoon	1½ tablespoons	2 tablespoons	2½ tablespoons	3 tablespoons
40 g (1½ oz)	65 g (2½ oz)	65 g (2½ oz)	75 g (3 oz)	100 g (4 oz)	150 g (5 oz)	175 g (6 oz)
90 g (3½ oz)	120 g (4½ oz)	175 g (6 oz)	225 g (8 oz)	375 g (13 oz)	425 g (15 oz)	500 g (1 lb 2 oz)
¼ teaspoon	½ teaspoon	¾ teaspoon	1 teaspoon	1½ teaspoons	2 teaspoons	2¼ teaspoons
¼ teaspoon	¼ teaspoon	½ teaspoon	¾ teaspoon	1¼ teaspoons	1½ teaspoons	1¾ teaspoons
good pinch	good pinch	good pinch	¼ teaspoon	½ teaspoon	¾ teaspoon	1 teaspoon

CHRISTMAS CAKE COUNTDOWN

14–20 days before: Apply almond paste (see chart page 134). Store in a cool, dry place for 4–5 days.
10–15 days before: Apply royal icing. Leave to dry for 1–2 days then apply second coat, again leaving to dry.
8–12 days before: Make the decorations for the cake.
7 days before: Complete all decorating a week before the cake is to be served.

ICING AND DECORATING THE CHRISTMAS CAKE

Royal icing is traditionally used to ice Christmas cake, and may be applied to give either a smooth surface, suitable for having piped and flat decoration added to it, or to make a rough 'snow-scene' effect. The latter is the easier way for the novice cake decorator and can look very good. See the Christmas cake illustrated on page 31.

Whichever way you decide to ice your cake, the surface and sides must first be covered with almond paste (marzipan) to provide a smooth surface to hold the Royal icing. This is available commercially, but home-made paste not only tastes better but is softer and easier to work with. However, if you are short of time and decide to buy almond paste, do not do so too far in advance: the fresher the paste is, the more pliable it will be.

QUANTITIES OF PASTE AND ICING FOR CHRISTMAS CAKE

The recipes given for almond paste and royal icing on the opposite page each yield 450 g (1 lb). Adjust the quantities according to the size of your cake, using the following chart as a guide to the amounts you will need:

SIZE	PASTE	ICING
13 cm (5 inch)	350 g (12 oz)	450 g (1 lb)
15 cm (6 inch)	450 g (1 lb)	500 g (1¼ lb)
18 cm (7 inch)	500 g (1¼ lb)	700 g (1½ lb)
20 cm (8 inch)	750 g (1¾ lb)	900 g (2 lb)
23 cm (9 inch)	900 g (2 lb)	1 kg (2¼ lb)
25 cm (10 inch)	1 kg (2¼ lb)	1.25 kg (2½ lb)
28 cm (11 inch)	1.25 kg (2½ lb)	1.4 kg (3 lb)
30 cm (12 inch)	1.5 kg (3 lb)	1.6 kg (3½ lb)

APPLYING ALMOND PASTE

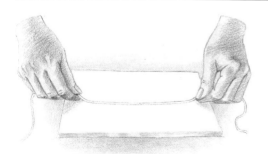

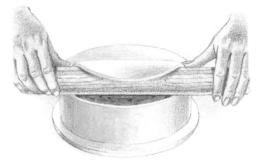

1. Measure round the cake with a piece of string. Dust board or work surface with icing sugar.

2. Roll out two-thirds of the paste to a rectangle measuring half the length of the string by twice the depth of the cake.

3. Trim the rectangle and cut in half lengthways.

4. Place the cake upside down on a board and brush the sides with warm apricot glaze.

5. Place the paste strips round the sides of the cake. Press lightly but firmly into position. Smooth joins with a palette knife.

6. Brush the top of the cake with apricot glaze and roll out the remaining paste to fit.

7. Using the rolling pin to help you, place the paste circle on top of the cake. Roll lightly to adhere, then smooth the join round the edge.

8. Wrap cake loosely in foil and store in a cool, dry place for 4–5 days before icing.

APRICOT GLAZE

This is used to help the almond paste adhere to the cake.
MAKES 150 ml (¼ pint)
100 g (4 oz) apricot jam

1. Put the apricot jam into a small saucepan with 2 tablespoons water and heat gently until dissolved. Bring to the boil, then simmer for 1 minute.
2. Use the glaze while still warm.

ALMOND PASTE

100 g (4 oz) icing sugar
100 g (4 oz) caster sugar
225 g (8 oz) ground almonds
few drops of almond essence (optional)
1–2 tablespoons lemon juice
1 egg, beaten

1. Sift the icing sugar into a bowl and stir in the caster sugar and ground almonds.
2. Add the almond essence if a more pronounced almond flavour is liked, and 1 tablespoon of the lemon juice. Work in the egg to form a stiff paste, adding more lemon juice if required. Form into a ball and knead lightly.

ROYAL ICING

2 egg whites
450 g (1 lb) icing sugar, sifted
1 teaspoon lemon juice
1 teaspoon glycerine

1. Whisk the egg whites in a bowl until slightly frothy. Stir in about 100 g (4 oz) of the icing sugar with a wooden spoon.
2. Gradually beat in the remaining sugar, beating well after each addition, and adding a little lemon juice and glycerine with each addition of sugar. The juice and glycerine will prevent the icing hardening.
3. Beat until the icing stands in soft peaks, then cover with a damp cloth and leave to stand for 1–2 hours, to allow any air bubbles to rise to the surface.

TO FLAT-ICE CHRISTMAS CAKE

1. Place the cake on a board, securing the base with a dab of icing. Stand on an icing turntable or upturned plate.
2. Put spoonfuls of about one-third of the icing on top of the cake.
Spread it evenly over the surface with a palette knife, using a paddling action.

3. Draw an icing ruler or palette knife evenly across the cake. Keep it at an angle of 30° and do not apply any pressure as you move it across the surface of the cake.

4. Neaten the edge by holding a palette knife upright and running it round the rim of the cake to remove surplus icing.
5. Leave to dry before icing the sides. Keep the icing in the bowl covered.
6. For a round cake, spread a thin, even layer of icing round the sides, using a palette knife with a paddling action.
7. Holding an icing comb or palette knife at an angle of 45° to the cake, move it slowly and evenly round the sides, rotating the cake slowly with your free hand. Lift any excess icing from the top of the cake and leave to dry.
8. For a square cake, ice two opposite sides first. Spread some icing on one side with a palette knife, then draw an icing comb or palette knife towards you, keeping the cake still. Cut off the icing down the corner in a straight line. Repeat with the opposite side and leave to dry, then ice the two remaining sides in the same way. Leave to dry, keeping the remaining icing covered.
9. When the cake is completely dry (this will take 1–2 days), thin the remaining icing with a little water and use to ice the top and sides of the cake as before. Leave to dry for a further 1–2 days before decorating.

TO ROUGH-ICE CHRISTMAS CAKE

Using this method, it is not necessary to apply 2 coats of icing. Or you could flat-ice the cake first, then rough-ice the sides only, leaving the top flat for decoration.
1. Using a palette knife, swirl Royal icing over the top and sides of the cake and spread out thickly, using a paddling action.
2. Using the palette knife, pull the icing up into 'peaks' to achieve the effect of a snow-scene.

TO FINISH THE CAKE

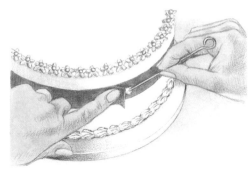

1. Place cake on cake board.

2. Use an icing bag fitted with an 8-point star nozzle to pipe a border round top edge.

3. Place a silver dragee in the centre of each piped star before the icing dries.

4. Using the same icing nozzle as for the top edge, pipe a shell border round the bottom edge.

5. Place Christmas cake ribbon round the edge, securing the join with a dab of icing.

6. Arrange holly leaves and Christmas roses on top.

CHRISTMAS CAKE DECORATIONS

Holly Leaves

1. Colour Almond paste dark green with green food colouring. Use red food colouring to colour a small quantity of paste a deep red.

2. Roll the green paste out thinly between 2 sheets of non-stick baking parchment.

3. Cut into small rectangles, then use the base of an icing nozzle to stamp out a holly leaf shape. Mark a centre vein with a small sharp knife and leave to dry.

4. Roll the red paste into tiny balls, to make berries. Arrange the holly leaves round clusters of berries.

These very attractive yet easy-to-make decorations for a Christmas cake can be made as much as 2 months in advance and stored in airtight containers, layered with greaseproof paper or non-stick baking parchment.

Christmas Roses

1. Roll out Almond paste (commercial white almond paste will give a good result) very thinly between 2 sheets of non-stick baking parchment.

2. Cut out 2 × 2 cm (½ inch) circles. Hold each circle at one side and press out until almost transparent.

3. Roll up the first circle for the centre of the rose and wrap the other one round it, to form a petal. It should be fairly tight at the base but left loose at the top to show the centre.

4. Make 3 more petals in the same way, pressing out each circle slightly larger than the previous one, and wrapping them round to form a full-blown rose. leave to dry.

CHRISTMAS DRINKS PARTIES

Inviting friends to share the festive spirit with you is very much part of Christmas – whether this is an impromptu get-together to wish each other the compliments of the season, or a more formal drinks party planned in advance.

There is a wide choice of drinks to suit every occasion and it's fun to come up with new ideas: Chapter 4 offers a useful selection of alcoholic and non-alcoholic drinks to inspire you.

The Mulled Wine recipe on page 106 would be an excellent festive choice for a Christmas drinks party.

You could also offer chilled white wine – always popular at drinks parties – as an alternative. Since not everybody likes a dry white wine, a hock would be a good choice here. Sparkling wine always gives a party special fizz, and you can achieve a sparkling but less alcoholic effect by mixing white wine with carbonated mineral water, to make a 'spritzer'. A 75-cl bottle of wine will yield approximately 6–8 glasses, and an allowance of about a half bottle per person is a fair rule of thumb for quantities. However, when ordering the wine for your party, you should also take into account that those guests who are driving will not be drinking. Incidentally, many wine shops and off licences have wine on a sale-or-return basis, and will hire out glasses for no more than a returnable deposit, charging only for breakages.

For the benefit of those who are keeping their alcohol intake low, remember to provide a good selection of interesting fruit juices, and plenty of mineral water. A mixture of fresh fruit juice and sparkling mineral water is a particularly refreshing combination.

Have a plentiful supply of ice cubes for adding to drinks: these can be stored in bags in the freezer.

FOOD TO SERVE WITH DRINKS

It is important to offer a good selection of nibbles at a drinks party, as it's not advisable to drink on an empty stomach. Apart from store-cupboard standbys like nuts, crisps, olives, cocktail onions and so on, the following cocktail snacks are easy to prepare:

Parma ham and melon balls: Scoop out balls from a seeded melon, wrap in strips of Parma ham and secure with cocktail sticks.

Smoked salmon pinwheels: Roll slices of brown bread with a rolling pin to make them more flexible for rolling up, then butter and remove crusts. Cover with sliced smoked salmon, roll up tightly, wrap in cling film and chill. Slice into thin rounds to serve. The rolls may be kept in the freezer. A very good way of making smoked salmon go further.

Mince pies: Tiny mince pies, served hot, are always popular at drinks parties.

Stuffed dates: Halve and stone fresh dates, then stuff with a mixture of cream cheese and grated Cheddar cheese, or with Brazil nuts.

Prawn cups: Fill tartlet cases, which can be made in advance and stored in an airtight tin, with prawns mixed with mayonnaise. Dust with paprika.

Bacon and prune skewers: Stuff pitted prunes with blanched almonds. Roll up in streaky bacon rashers, secure with wooden cocktail sticks and grill under a hot grill.

Celery boats: Cut celery stalks into 3.5 cm ($1\frac{1}{2}$ inch) lengths. Fill with blue cheese mashed with a little thick yogurt.

Avocado dip: Purée 1 large or 2 medium peeled and stoned avocado pears in a blender. Add 100 g (4 oz) curd cheese, 2 tablespoons yogurt, 1 tablespoon finely chopped spring onion, 1 teaspoon lemon juice and a dash of Tabasco and purée again until smooth and creamy. Check the seasoning. Cover the purée with cling film if not using immediately.

Cheese and pineapple sticks: Cut a selection of cheeses, such as smoked Cheddar, Red Leicester, Gouda, into cubes. Peel, core and cube a fresh pineapple or use canned pineapple chunks in natural juice. Spear a cheese cube and a pineapple cube with a cocktail stick.

Artichoke hearts with anchovy cream: Drain a can of artichoke hearts and fill with a mixture of cream or curd cheese mixed with finely chopped anchovies.

ALTERNATIVE CHRISTMAS

Taking a break from a conventional Christmas and ringing the changes on tradition can be every bit as festive. The vegetarian menu proves that Christmas dinner without meat can be delicious, and although Christmas often means cooking for a crowd, Christmas dinner for just the two of you will be a memorable occasion with our romantic menu.

VEGETARIAN CHRISTMAS DINNER FOR FOUR

PINK FRUIT COCKTAILS
2 pink grapefruit
175 g (6 oz) red grapes
1 small Charentais melon
1 pomegranate

1. Peel and segment the grapefruits, removing all the pith.
2. Halve and seed the grapes.
3. Halve and seed the melon and scoop the flesh into balls, using a melon-baller.
4. Mix the fruits in a bowl, then spoon into individual glasses. Cut the pomegranate in half, and sprinkle the fruit cocktails with the juice and seeds. Serve chilled.

CHRISTMAS NUT ROAST
40 g (1½ oz) butter
2–3 tablespoons dried breadcrumbs
1 onion, peeled and chopped
50 g (2 oz) hazelnuts, grated or chopped
50 g (2 oz) cashew nuts, grated or very finely chopped
50 g (2 oz) Brazil nuts, grated or chopped
50 g (2 oz) ground almonds
100 g (4 oz) fresh wholemeal breadcrumbs
4 tablespoons milk
2 eggs, beaten
salt and black pepper
freshly grated nutmeg
Stuffing:
100 g (4 oz) butter, softened
grated rind and juice of ½ lemon
1 teaspoon dried mixed herbs
4 tablespoons finely chopped parsley
2 spring onions, very finely chopped
100 g (4 oz) fresh wholemeal breadcrumbs

To garnish:
2 tablespoons chopped hazelnuts, toasted

1. Line a 23 × 13 × 7.5 cm (9 × 5 × 3 inch) loaf tin with non-stick baking parchment. Grease with 15 g (½ oz) of the butter, then sprinkle with the breadcrumbs, to coat evenly.
2. Melt the remaining butter in a frying pan, add the onion and fry over a gentle heat for about 7 minutes or until soft and lightly browned. Mix with all the remaining roast ingredients in a bowl, stirring well to combine.
3. Make the stuffing: cream the butter in a bowl, then gradually work in all the remaining stuffing ingredients, until well blended.
4. Spoon half the nut mixture into the prepared tin, pressing it down well with the back of the spoon. Spread with the stuffing mixture, then top with the remaining nut mixture, spreading it out evenly and pressing down well. Cover with buttered foil.
5. Bake in a preheated oven, 180°C, 350°F, Gas Mark 4, for 1 hour. Remove the foil and return to the oven for 5–10 minutes. Remove from the oven and leave to stand in the tin for 5 minutes.
6. Very carefully turn out on to a heated serving dish and gently remove the lining paper. Sprinkle with chopped toasted hazelnuts to serve. Serve cut into slices, with Cranberry sauce (page 19) and with vegetables, such as Brussels sprouts and leek purée.

BRUSSELS SPROUTS AND LEEK PURÉE
450 g (1 lb) Brussels sprouts, trimmed
4 leeks, cut into short lengths
25 g (1 oz) butter
4 tablespoons double cream
ground nutmeg
salt and black pepper

1. Cook the Brussels sprouts and leeks in separate pans of boiling salted water until tender. Drain very thoroughly then blend together to a smooth purée with the butter and cream.
2. Season to taste with nutmeg, salt and pepper. Reheat very gently to serve.

VEGETARIAN CHRISTMAS PUDDING
Makes 2 × 600 ml (1 pint) puddings.
225 g (8 oz) dates, stoned and chopped
150 ml (¼ pint) rum
225 g (8 oz) butter, softened
175 g (6 oz) soft dark brown sugar
2 eggs, lightly beaten
2 tablespoons black treacle
grated rind and juice of 1 lemon
100 g (4 oz) raisins
100 g (4 oz) cut mixed peel
25 g (1 oz) blanched almonds, chopped
225 g (8 oz) currants
100 g (4 oz) sultanas
100 g (4 oz) plain wholemeal flour
100 g (4 oz) fresh wholemeal breadcrumbs
½ teaspoon freshly grated nutmeg
½ teaspoon ground ginger
1½ teaspoons mixed spice

1. Put the dates and rum into a small heavy saucepan and simmer gently until soft. Remove from the heat and allow to cool.
2. Cream the butter with the sugar in a mixing bowl, then stir in the date mixture followed by the eggs, treacle, lemon rind and juice. Mix well, then gradually stir in all the remaining ingredients, to give a soft dropping consistency.

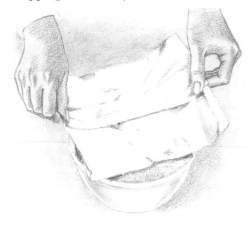

3. Spoon the mixture into 2 × 600 ml (1 pint) greased pudding basins. Cover with pleated greased greaseproof paper and foil. Tie securely with string.
4. Place each basin in a saucepan and pour in boiling water to come halfway up the sides. Steam for 4 hours, topping up with more boiling water as necessary.
5. Store the puddings in a cool, dry place, away from direct sunlight.
6. Steam for a further 3 hours before serving, turned out, with brandy butter, or cream, or custard.

CHRISTMAS DINNER FOR TWO

What could be more festive than wild duck served in a really special sauce of black cherries enriched with port? Smoked salmon wrapped round a filling of smoked trout pâté makes an interesting and unusual starter. Finish off the meal on a seasonal note with a creamy syllabub made with stem ginger.

SMOKED SALMON AND TROUT PARCELS
2 trout fillets
50 g (2 oz) curd cheese
2 teaspoons horseradish cream
finely grated rind and juice of ½ lemon
freshly ground black pepper
4 slices smoked salmon
To garnish:
lemon slices
watercress sprigs

1. To make the filling, mash the trout fillets in a bowl with a fork. Beat in the curd cheese, horseradish cream and lemon rind and juice. Season with pepper.
2. Spoon a quarter of the smoked trout mixture on to the centre of each smoked salmon slice. Wrap the smoked salmon round to form a parcel, then place seam side down on individual serving plates. Garnish with lemon slices and watercress sprigs. Serve with brown bread and butter.

WILD DUCK WITH BLACK CHERRY SAUCE
2 wild ducks
75 g (3 oz) butter
salt and black pepper
1 shallot, finely chopped
1 × 225 g (8 oz) can stoned black cherries
100 ml (3½ fl oz) chicken stock
300 ml (½ pint) port
2 tablespoons redcurrant jelly
1 bay leaf
1 teaspoon cornflour

1. Rub the ducks all over with 50 g (2 oz) of the butter. Season inside and out with salt and pepper. Roast in the oven at 200°C, 400°F, Gas Mark 6 for about 45 minutes, or until cooked through.
2. Meanwhile, melt the remaining butter in a medium saucepan and fry the shallot gently until soft but not coloured. Drain the cherries, reserving the fruit, and add the juice to the pan together with the stock, port and redcurrant jelly. Heat, stirring, until the jelly has dissolved, then add the bay leaf and simmer for about 20 minutes.
3. Remove the bay leaf. Mix the cornflour with a little water, to make a smooth paste, and stir into the pan. Heat gently, stirring, until the sauce is thickened and smooth. Season to taste with salt and pepper. Stir in the reserved cherries.
4. Cut each cooked duck in half and place on a heated serving platter. Pour half the Black cherry sauce over the ducks and hand the remaining sauce separately in a sauce boat. Serve accompanied by roast potatoes and steamed broccoli spears.

GINGER SYLLABUB
150 ml (¼ pint) double cream
100 ml (3½ fl oz) avocaat
4 tablespoons chopped stem ginger, with some of the syrup, or 4 tablespoons ginger marmalade

1. Whip the cream until it stands in soft peaks. Fold in the avocaat, then the ginger.
2. Spoon the mixture into glasses and serve chilled, accompanied by crisp biscuits, such as the Spiced Christmas Cookies on page 120.

MENU PLANNER

CHRISTMAS EVE SUPPER

Chestnut Soup: page 33

Baked Halibut Parcels: page 41

Wine Jelly: page 77

CHRISTMAS MORNING BRUNCH

Smoked Haddock Mousse: page 38

Cold Game Pie or Small Mutton Pies: page 65

Christmas Bread: page 10

Dried Fruit Salad: page 66

TRADITIONAL CHRISTMAS DINNER

Game Soup with Lentils: page 30

Roast Turkey with Bread Sauce: page 28

Brussels Sprouts with Chestnuts: page 26

Christmas Pudding: page 30

Brandy Butter: page 9

BOXING DAY LUNCH

Seviche of Scallops: page 38

Carbonade Flamande: page 50

Cinnamon Apple Charlotte: page 68

BOXING DAY TEA

Traditional Christmas Cake: page 30

Ginger Thins: page 120

Spiced Christmas Cookies: page 120

Gingerbread: page 70

NEW YEAR'S EVE SUPPER

Turbot Gratin: page 42

Glazed Baked Ham: page 58

Fresh Fruit Salad: page 74

NEW YEAR'S DAY LUNCH

Smoked Salmon Pâté: page 36

Roast Venison: page 49

Raspberry Meringue: page 78

EPIPHANY LUNCH

Parsnip Soup: page 36

Braised Pheasant: page 65

Blazing Apples: page 68

VEGETARIAN CELEBRATION MEAL

Herb Soufflé: page 42

Vegetarian Casserole: page 62

Mince Pies: page 20

INDEX

ACKNOWLEDGEMENTS

Photography
VERNON MORGAN

Photographic styling
MARIAN PRICE

Preparation of food for photography
ALLYSON BIRCH

Illustrations
HEATHER JANE DAVIES

Step-by-Step Illustrations
PATRICIA CAPON

Other pictures in this book are reproduced with permission of the following:
Bridgeman Art·Library: Christopher Wood Gallery 6, Hirsch Sprungske Collection, Copenhagen, 24, 54.
Mary Evans Picture Library: 10 bottom left, 19 bottom right, 72.
Fine Art Photographic Library: 80, 94, 104, 112, 114.